SMART

MONEY

Your Simple Guide to
Understanding Bonds

JOHN ENDRIS

ISBN-13: 978-1978112704

ISBN-10: 197811270X

TABLE OF CONTENTS

INTRODUCTION

Despite the importance of finance, accounting, and consumer intelligence, these topics are typically neglected in high schools. Unfortunately, personal finance is often learned by trial and error. The problem with this method of learning is that it only takes one costly financial mishap to set you back for years. This is why I created the *Smart Money* series. With the concepts I these books you can learn what fits your financial objectives and what to avoid.

I grew up in extreme poverty, and discovered how to be disciplined with money because my limited funds needed to go a long way. Without any guidance, I was left to learn by trial and error, and like most people, I made plenty of costly mistakes. Over the years I had several credit cards, got an investment account, bought a car and a house. Since I studied finance in college and have spent almost a decade as a finance professional, I now know exactly how the system works and want to help you avoid all of the "gotchas."

Unfortunately, for decades the financial industry has gotten rich from misinformation, legal manipulation, calculated exploitation, and naive customers. Financial insiders use the term "smart money" to describe an informed and savvy investor, and "dumb money" to describe the opposite side of the trade. In most markets the smart money will absorb the dumb money.

This book will not tell you what to invest in (the economy is not static). Instead it will teach you how to figure out what works well for you. Once you discover how to operate like the *smart money*, the only time you will transfer your earnings willfully is to fund your own enterprise. My aim with the books in this series is to save you time and expensive pain by teaching you financial concepts that you can use to make your life better, create a brighter future, and become the smart money.

Rather than use highbrow financial acronyms and other barrier jargon, I have tried to be as informal and succinct as possible. At times I even attempt sarcasm to bring some levity to this serious subject. Most of the valuable secrets I am willfully sharing with you are things you can use for your entire life, and things I wish someone had shared with me. I am excited to share these secrets and am happy you decided to learn how the system works.

This book is not meant to turn you into a bond trader or an experienced portfolio manager. In fact, I recommend that you have a professional manage your money. However, knowing how to evaluate and assess how bonds fit into your personal financial goals is important. Not only will you be able to understand your portfolio composition, you will also be able to figure out what best fits your risk profile and financial goals. The focus of this book is self-empowerment, so by the end you will be the smart money.

This book begins by describing what bonds are and the basic fundamentals. The next portion is dedicated to teaching you about underwriting in the primary market, and how trading in the secondary market works. The final chapters will teach you what to look for, what to avoid, and how to move to the next level with your personal strategy. Of course, there is also an entire section dedicated to useful terminology that you can reference at any time.

At first, finance seems complicated, but I purposely made the chapters short, so you can read them again if you need to. In fact, this book is one that you will be able to read in one sitting, and probably more than once. If at any time you need help with any terminology just go to the *Fundamental Terms* section. After this book, you will be able to use this knowledge to implement the financial secrets I share. Being the smart money will likely change your life, so let's begin.

WHAT IS A BOND?

Bond, James Bond. I know, super corny, but I could not help it. Everyone is obsessed with the stock market and the financial news never stops discussing every detail. However, if you have any kind of managed fund it is 99% likely that you own some bonds and probably don't even know it. Bonds remain an enigma, the secret agent of finance that is always present, but somehow never noticed. So why should you care?

Capitalism is an expansionist system built on constant growth, which often relies on the capital markets. Whether you like it or not, this system exists to provide mutual benefits for those that need funding and those that can provide it. Therefore, having a basic understanding of how the market can benefit an investor or a business, creates a mutual benefit for both entities and diminishes exploitation.

First, let's imagine you are a firm that needs funding for a major initiative. What are your options? Strip away any excess expenses, and sell as many assets as you can to raise cash? Try to issue some shares (if you are listed) to investors on a public exchange? Get a loan from a bank? Or issue bonds? All of which are possible, which option do you select?

Cutting too deeply or selling assets can diminish productivity, so this is often not the best option for a firm or an investor. Of course, any publicly traded firm can create more equities/stock and then sell those on a public exchange for cash. However, adding new shares makes the existing ones less valuable, which annoys investors. In fact, *diluting* shareholder value can sometimes trigger investors to sell instead of buy. Plus, there may not even be enough market demand to support the firm's financing needs.

A firm can use a bank loan for funding, but that will typically be accompanied by a restrictive *covenant*. Not meeting the covenant's specific requirement (like quarterly revenue projections) may force the firm to pay more in interest, or sell some assets to support the loan. Bank covenants have a reputation for being strict and unforgiving. Selling shares or getting a loan has mixed benefits for the firm and also the investor.

That leaves selling bonds. There are plenty of mutual benefits in this arrangement because a bond is a loan from an investor instead of a bank. Like any loan, a bond contract pays interest on a fixed schedule and repays the principal to the investor at a stated time. Issuing debt (bonds) instead of equity (stocks) is referred to as *leverage financing* because the issuer is borrowing against its net worth (quantifiable) and not its equity (fluctuating).

Why is the bond market something that you should care about? First, the bond market has always been twice the size of the stock market, yet it is often ignored. Therefore, if you know how to find deals, there is far less competition for those. Second, bonds are predictable and stable. With stocks, there is no guaranteed return and no matter how much risk you accept you can still take a loss. Third, with bonds, you can directly invest in initiatives that matter to you.

To issue a bond a firm hires to a bank to do the underwriting and to manage the cash flow. When the due diligence is done, the lead/agented bank creates an individual bond number called a *Committee on Uniform Securities Identification* (CUSIP) number that an investor can buy. Essentially, this is just creating a loan, but breaking that loan up into small parcels and selling those individually. Therefore, you buy an individual bond and the CUSIP belongs to you until you either sell it, the firm retires it, or it matures.

Bonds are created in the primary market by bankers (underwriting), and sold to investors in the secondary market (public exchanges). The benefit of a bond is that a firm gets immediate cash, and can set its own terms. For an investor, the company will fully repay you and you can charge interest for the money you lent out. Obviously, you must agree to their terms, or what the market defines, but overall it is generally a mutually beneficial arrangement.

If you buy a bond you are a bank. You will have a term, a coupon, a maturity date, a credit rating, and a spread to deal with. However, that is a good thing. Unfortunately, with stocks you have none of those things, and due to the unpredictability of the terms (no terms) your risk is always much higher. The terms for bonds are generally favorable for both the investor and also the firm, or there would never be any buyers.

The bond market is so much larger because an investor can buy a bond from a corporation, a sovereign/government, or a municipality/city. Even though there is a variety of bonds available, everything you need to know is in this book. An idealistic tenet of mine that I hold dear is that there should be economic equality for everyone.

This does not mean that everyone should be rich. It means that everyone should have an equal chance, and I believe that opportunity comes with knowledge. Like all of the other books in the *Smart Money* series my objective is not to provide exact investments (give you a fish). Instead this book is meant to empower you to assess and select investments that fit your circumstances and personal goals (teach you how to fish). Therefore, each chapter will have an action item that will help you do some discovery of your own.

ACTION ITEM

The bond market is literally the largest securities market in the world and has limitless options. According to visual capitalist, all five major stock exchanges in North America have a combined value of 28 Billion. All 17 exchanges in Europe are have a combined value of 13 Billion. All 60 stock exchanges on the planet have a combined value of 69 trillion. The 2016 global bond market was estimated at 100 trillion. As you can see, bonds are a big deal.

Go to MorningStar.com and check out any recognizable firm. All you have to do is type in the firms name into the quote box at the top. On the bottom set of the firm's tabs you will see a "bonds" tab on the far right. Towards the top of this tab you will find the amount of debt and equity listed. At the bottom look over some the bond's coupons (interest paid). Then take a moment and reflect.

Look at the difference between Ford (F), Sears (SHLD), and Tenet (TNT). What are the coupons (interest) the firm had to pay to investors? Were some of those coupons higher than others? Were all the bonds maturities spread out or due at the same time? By the end of this book, you will know how to evaluate issuers, so practicing this basic search will become extremely valuable.

BOND FUNDAMENTALS

There are some basic characteristics that all bonds share. Therefore, learning about these now will make this book easy to use and understand. Overall, all bonds are identified by three things:

1. Issuer: Who must repay the lender.
2. Coupon Rate: Interest paid on a loan.
3. Maturity: The date the repayment is due.

Unfortunately, bond jargon makes the simplicity of this structure seem more complex. A "Ford fives of 20" is a bond issued by Ford Motor company, with 5% interest that will be repaid in 2020. That bond's face value (amount paid at maturity) is called the *par value*. The legal document that contains all of the details/terms of the bond issuance is called the *indenture*. For the issuer, the payment terms set are usually one of these nine things:

1. Interest only: The periodic payments are only the coupons, then at maturity the principal is paid off.

2. Sinking fund: Periodic payments are made, but the issuer sets aside money in a separate custodial account for the exclusive purpose of retiring a portion of the bonds.

3. Balloon: Often bonds are issued to mature in intervals, bonds in a term issue that have the same maturity date are called balloon.

4. Income: A rare arrangement where only the face value of the bond is promised to be paid. Any coupon payments get paid, only if the issuer has enough earnings to do so.

5. Annuity: Pays out a fixed stream of payments at agreed upon intervals.

6. Zero Coupon: An *accrual* bond that does not pay a coupon, but is bought at a steep discount. The profit comes at maturity when the bond is redeemed at full face value.

7. Variable Rate: The coupon *floats* and is usually based on LIBOR or the Fed funds rate with a quoted spread added that is fixed.

8. Perpetual: Like a stock dividend. This type of payment has no maturity date, are not redeemable, and have a steady stream of payments. (Also known as "perps") This kind of arrangement is rare because there are very few entities that are safe enough to issue bonds that will never be repaid.

9. <u>Convertible</u>: Bonds like this can be converted to stock. A variation of this is where the bond can be exchanged for stock from a different firm (used in some mergers and acquisitions).

Generally, the payment terms listed above terms are set by the issuer, and then accepted by the investor. Those terms are fixed and cannot be changed unless the bond is retired/paid off in full. A bond can also be *secured* with revenue or collateral of some kind or *unsecured* where it is not backed or is supported by the taxing power of a municipality. Those factors combined with short or long term maturities, or staggered terms are the basic features of bond contracts.

Interest is earned for each day that a bond is held, but interest (coupon) payments are generally made twice a year only. If the bond is sold before maturity, the bond buyer must pay the *accrued interest* to the seller of the bond. However, the accrued interest is calculated using a 360 day year.

I bet that most of what was just mentioned sounds like some boring on-boarding material for your new job at a bank. However, all of those things become easy to conceptualize if you think of a bond as a loan. Therefore, what you learned here will be quite useful when combined with the rest of the material in this book.

ACTION ITEM

One of the simplest, yet most confusing things for people who don't have a background in finance is bond pricing. The coupon is the periodic interest payment that the bondholder receives during the time when the bond is issued and when it matures. The coupon will always remain constant, but the price of the bond can change.

As an investor you will almost always get back your original investment with a bond. However, it is normal for a bond's price to fluctuate. A bond can sell at *par*, at a *discount,* or at a *premium*. For now, just remember that *par* is what the bond sold for when it was issued. A bond selling at a *discount* is one that sells for lower than the par value, and a bond selling at a *premium* sells for a higher price than it did at par.

If you want, you can do some experimentation with a bond yield calculator at www.money-zine.com/calculators/investment-calculators/bond-yield-calculator/. Typically, bonds are sold with a face value of $1,000.00. So key in $1,000.00 for the bond's price, and $1,000.00 for the par value. Put in 5% for the coupon, 2 years to maturity, and then calculate. Notice how the *bond yield* and *yield to maturity* (YTM) are the same?

Keep everything the same, except this time analyze a discount bond by putting in $900.00 into the bond's price box. Notice how the bond yield went up, and the yield to maturity doubled? Keep everything the same except now, but this time try a premium by putting in $1,100.00 into the bond price box. Notice how the yield went way down and the YTM became non-existent?

The *current bond yield* is the rate of interest paid to the bond holder, and the *yield to maturity* is the total yield if it is held to maturity. The increase or decrease in yield compensates for the price change, which technically makes the bond equal to its original par value. Therefore, there is a good reason for the changes you witnessed. Hopefully, this experiment made you curious to read the next chapter, which explains why price changes occur.

BOND PRICING

Like loans, bonds are simple in theory, but mired in complex terms. However, once you understand how bonds work, that jargon will all make sense. Hopefully, you did the action item in the last chapter and still are curious about why a bond's price would change. That example might be confusing, but I know you will get this concept immediately once you learn the details. Bond pricing seems complex, but it is actually quite simple.

The price of a bond is usually stated as a percentage of its par value. In the previous example, a bond with a price of $1,000.00 is selling for 100% of its par value of $1,000.00. A bond selling at $900.00 is selling at a discount equal to 90% of its $1,000.00 par value (90%*1,000). A bond selling at $1,100.00 is selling at a premium, equivalent to 110% of its $1,000.00 par value (10%*1,000). This part is probably quite straight forward.   From the action item you probably ascertained that prices and yields move in opposite directions. When the bond was discounted the yield went up, and when the bond was at a premium the yield went down. If someone could buy an otherwise identical bond with a 5% yield, why would they buy an older bond with a 3% yield? Therefore, the bond's price must fall to bring the yield to a level where the investor will want to own that bond.

A bond trades at a premium when its coupon rate is higher than the prevailing interest rates because there is more demand for it. A bond trades at a discount when its coupon rate is lower than the interest rate and there is less demand for it. Typically, there will be a higher proportion of bonds trading at a premium during times of falling rates, because and more discounted bonds in periods of rising rates because when interest rates are rising because new bonds will pay investors higher interest rates than old ones.

The key is to recognize that a bond's price reflects the value of the income that it provides through its regular coupon interest payments. When prevailing interest rates fall, investors holding older bonds with higher rates can charge a *premium* to sell those in the secondary market. On the other hand, if interest rates rise, older bonds may become less valuable because their coupons are relatively low, and older bonds will trade at a *discount.*

Traditionally, bonds move in the opposite direction of interest rates. When interest rates rise, bonds fall, and vice versa. If you buy a bond and hold it until it matures, swings in interest rates and the resulting swings in the bond's price won't matter. But if you sell your bond before it matures, the price it fetches will be largely related to the interest rate environment. Investors who study bond pricing, can trade bonds for a profit.

Typically, long term bond's prices will fluctuate more

than short term bond's prices, and the yields of short term bonds will fluctuate more than those for long term bonds. This happens because issuers bringing new short term bonds to the marketplace will have to pay higher rates of interest. The rates of long term will usually change slower. As mentioned before, if there are new bonds pay higher coupons, the demand for older issues with lower rates falls.

Bond pricing uses *basis points* to describe changes. Each 1% is known as a point. If a bond price changes from 90 to 91 it has increased by one point. However, the actual price has increased from $900.00 (90% of 1,000 face value) to $910.00 (91% of 1,000) Therefore, the value of the point is actually $10.00, 1/4 point is $2.50, a 1/2 point is $5.00. To anyone not in the finance industry, a point probably seems like a silly way to describe this. However, to a banker a *basis point* is crucial terminology.

Just like stocks, bonds can be bought and sold in the *secondary market* after being issued. While some bonds are traded publicly through exchanges, most trade over the counter between large broker-dealers acting on their client's or their own behalf. A bond's price and yield determine its value in the secondary market. *Yield* is based on the purchase price of the bond as well as the coupon.

The easiest way to understand bond prices is to add a zero to the price quoted in the market. For example, if a bond is quoted at 99 in the market, the price is $990.00 for every $1,000.00 of face value. If this were the case, the bond is said to be trading at a *discount*. If the bond is trading at 101, it costs $1,010.00 for every $1,000.00 of face value. Therefore, the bond would be at a *premium*. If the bond is trading at 100, it costs $1,000.00 for every $1,000.00 of face value. So it would be trading at par.

On a short-term basis, falling interest rates can boost the value of bonds in a portfolio and rising rates may hurt its value. However, over the long term rising interest rates can actually increase a bond portfolio's return as the money from maturing bonds is reinvested in bonds with higher yields. Conversely, in a falling interest rate environment, money from maturing bonds may need to be reinvested in new bonds that pay lower rates, potentially lowering longer-term returns.

ACTION ITEM

Now that you know why bonds change prices and how that affects the yield I am sure you are thinking about trading. Most everyone understands that firms or individuals with a higher risk of default must pay more interest for credit. This is why lower quality bonds always have a higher yield, and are also more affected by pricing. However, be mindful that the most common mistake that investors make is reaching for too much yield.

Chasing yield is a common avoidable mistake, but so is failing to find the best prices. Often bonds will have broker commissions built into the price. Depending on the demand, this markup will vary. After you read this book you will have real industry insight, but no real trading experience. Obviously, you can't become a bond trader after reading a book. However, you can now negotiate a fair price, which is what trading is all about.

I encourage you to look at daily prices on several sites. If you do this action item you will often see that brokers will list the same bond for different prices. Obviously, you should never pay more than most recently traded price so don't be afraid to negotiate. Before you do so, do some research because due to the size of the market the broker will not know what the particular bond is worth.

The action plan here is that if you act like a pro you will be treated like a pro. Look up the CUSIP of the bond you want to buy, or at least know what the market is doing.

Fidelity has a great CUSIP tool for this. You can also use Schwab's research tools as well. For now, I suggest you experiment with those tools, but at least read the rest of the book before making any trades or attempting to become a serious bond trader.

MATURITY

Another important factor to consider about bonds besides price, and the coupon, is the maturity. The maturity date is the day on which the issuer must pay the principal (face value) of the bond to the investor. The investor will also receive their last semi-annual interest payment. To find the maturity for any bond listed is quite simple, a maturity date of 6-1-21 matures on June 1, 2021. What more is there to learn about maturity?

As a bond investor, you should know that there is more risk of default with a longer maturity than there is with shorter one. Therefore, the longer the maturity is the higher the coupon usually is. In the marketplace, the prices on longer term bonds are also usually more volatile than shorter term bonds. Just so there is no confusion about how coupon rates fit with maturity here is a quick example of a bond you might buy:

10% coupon
$1,000.00 denomination
6-1-2018 Maturity

A 10% bond would receive $100.00 a year (10%*1,000) bonds typically pay interest semiannually, for this example the investor would receive two payments of $50.00 each

The maturity rate determines the rate of the interest payments. The issuer pays interest on the anniversary of the bonds maturity date and six months from the date of maturity. Since the date in the example above is 6/1/2018, that bond will pay interest on June 1 and December 1 each year until the bond matures. If you bought this in 2017 these $50.00 semi-annual payments would continue until 2018. Then at maturity, you would get the $1,000.00 face value back and claim the $100.00 you received in coupons as profit.

Depending on the credit rating of the bond, the returns are quite dependable. Unless you buy a "zero." *Zero coupon bonds* can be issued by corporations, municipalities, and also by the Federal government. Unlike regular bonds, zeroes do not pay interest at regular intervals and there are no coupons. Instead, the investor purchases the bond at a deep discount from par value. The difference between the purchase price and the amount the investor receives when the bond matures is the interest (referred to as "residual").

You can buy municipal or corporate zero coupon bonds, but the most common ones are from the U.S. Treasury. Just like any other bond, a zero has a credit rating done by the big three agencies (Moodys, S&P, Fitch). Zeroes are also called, "muni-savers" or "strips." Separate

Trading of Registered Interest and Principal Securities (STRIPS) are popular because a financial institution or a government securities broker can convert an eligible Treasury security into a strip. Just like regular bonds the denominations will be $1,000.00.

This is a "buy low sell high" investment where you purchase the zero much lower than the face value. Therefore, you want to get the deepest discount that you can. Usually, the longer the period until the bond matures, the deeper the discount. Often when the interest rates are low, the prices of zeroes will be higher, but when the interest rates are high the zero will discounted more. Zero coupon bonds can be bought through most full or discount brokers, financial intermediaries, or commercial banks.

As mentioned previously, bonds with longer maturities, also have higher coupon rates. If your money is tied up for a longer period of time, you should expect a higher rate of return. Longer term bonds also tend to fluctuate more than those with shorter maturities. A change in interest rates will affect the prices of a 30 year bond than a 5 year bond, and zeroes are even more sensitive to changes in interest rates than regular bonds are.

A strength of the zero is that you can lock in the *yield to maturity* (YTM) and you can get great deals on discounted bonds. The one problem with zeros is how the I.R.S. handles the investment. Capital gains tax is paid on the return of an investment, but zeroes are taxed like income (a higher rate). Even though you don't collect the accumulated income/return until the bond matures, you have to pay taxes on it as if it is invisible income. With no coupon, then why would you want to buy this?

Investors who desire a lump sum payment at some future date will find this arrangement appealing. Let's say you need $20K in 2018 to pay for a child's first year of college. In 2000 you bought a zero with the par value of 20K. This was scheduled to mature in 2018. At the time you paid $5K for the bonds, but you wouldn't receive the interest payment until the bonds mature in 2018, when you finally received the 20K. A popular strategy used to diversify credit risk is to *ladder* zeroes by purchasing several smaller bonds with different maturity dates rather than one large bond with a single maturity rate.

ACTION ITEM

Utilizing a staggered bond portfolio composed of several different maturities provides liquidity and lessens credit default risk. Having some zeroes in your portfolio may be suitable for your investment needs. Use a zero coupon calculator (www.miniwebtool.com/zero-coupon-bond-calculator/) so you can get an idea about how the discounts work. What you will discover right away is that the longer the maturity, the greater the discount. If you are feeling ambitious and want to learn how to compare equivalent YTM for a zero coupon bond, use this wiki to learn the basic calculations.

Despite bonds having a predictable payout, and a transparent credit rating, there are still risks. With any investment, the higher the risk, the greater the yield will be. With certain types of bonds, there is greater risk than others. Even if you researched the issuer, the coupon, and the maturity you still have to consider risk. What types of risk do you have to consider? After reading the next chapter you can definitely add another tool to your bond investment toolbox.

TYPES OF RISK

Overall, bonds are one of the safest ways to invest because the payout is fixed and contractually guaranteed. In fact, you probably own bonds right now and don't even know it. Unlike stocks, bond payments never change and even if a firm goes bankrupt, bond holders are still made whole. Plus, stocks always change price and are subject to massive swings up or down. In comparison, bonds are boring, but like all investments there is some type of risk.

Every bond will have a rating which is usually based on a firm's ability to pay it back. The bond rating system helps investors determine a firm's credit risk and coupon in the market. A bond's rating is suggested by the "underwriters" (the bank that created it) then confirmed or changed by the "big three" rating agencies (Moody's, S&P, and Fitch) Below are the ratings a bond can have:

AAA: *Investment grade, highest quality*
AA: *Investment grade, high quality*
A: *Investment grade, strong*
BBB: *Investment grade, medium grade*
BB: *Junk, speculative*
B: *Junk, speculative*
CCC/CC/C: *Junk, highly speculative*
D: *Junk, in default*

Investment grade will have the least risk, but the lowest coupon. As the rating worsens from A-D the risk increases, but with that so does the coupon. Junk bonds may or may not default, and often those can be bought at a discount. Depending on your portfolio and investment objective, junk bonds may fit. If you were to look at your current portfolio in a typical 401K you will see a variety of bonds. Usually, AAA-BBB, and US Treasuries are the safest investment.

Rating agencies regularly review bond ratings every 6-12 months, but can also be reviewed at any time an agency deems necessary. Especially, if payments are missed, or the issuer's underlying financial position drastically changes. This does happen, but very rarely. In fact, the reason why bonds are intermingled with stocks in a portfolio is because unlike stocks, a bond's return is predictable and steady.

Title 12, Chapter VII, Subchapter A, Part 709, Section 709.5, and *Bankruptcy Code 507* states exactly what will occur if a firm goes under and must default on its debt. Why is this important? If this were to happen, *liquidation rights* are pre-established. Wages, obligations, and taxes are paid first, then secured debt (loans and bonds). If there is money left over after liquidation unsecured debt is paid (common stock and preferred shares). Therefore, even if you own just one bond, you get paid before biggest shareholder. Yet there are still risk factors to consider.

The type of rating on a bond defines only one kind of risk. Reinvestment, event, interest rate, sector, call, marketability, default and liquidity risk are additional risk factors to consider when selecting the right bond for your portfolio. Aren't bonds supposed to be safe, boring, and predictable? Overall, bonds are stable investments, but nothing is perfect. These types of risk exist in varying degree no matter what type of investment you are considering.

Reinvestment risk is very common. Since you don't know where future rates are going to be you cannot be certain if you can find a similar yield at maturity. When the bond matures, interest rates could have fallen from where you bought the original bond, thus giving you lower income from a new bond. This risk is something that bond investors are always conscious of.

Imagine you bought a $25,000.00 10 year municipal bond (tax free) with 10% interest coupon (25,000*0.10) you would get $2,500.00 a year from it. Now that 10 years have passed and that bond was redeemed, the new issue only has a 5% interest/coupon rate. The 5% coupon on the new issue would only yield you $1,250.00 (25,000*0.05). In this scenario you lost $1,250.00 in income from that bond (2,500-1,250). This is an example of reinvestment risk.

Event risk is exactly what it sounds like. An unpredictable catastrophe, which could be a natural disaster, a massive fraud, or a product recall. Any significant event that disrupts the cash flow of the issuer will inevitably affect the bond's price in the market. A less obvious event risk is when a strong firm merges with a weak one. In this scenario, the weaker firm's bonds could get upgraded, which will change the price.

By far the biggest risk for bonds is usually *interest rate risk*. This could also be called "market risk." Just in case you forgot. Interest rate changes impact a bond's value, but not the coupon. The bond's value typically falls as interest rates rise because its lower interest rates makes it less appealing to investors. Regardless of interest rate risk, the coupon rate is guaranteed and does not change.

As explained in the previous chapters, bond prices are sensitive to interest rates. Traditionally when interest rates go down, bond prices go up and when interest rates go up, bond prices go down. Typically, the price will fall until the yield is the same level as the new yield levels for similar bonds. Bonds with longer maturities are usually more vulnerable to interest rate risk. By now you are fully aware that this type of risk is fundamental to a bond investor's decisions.

Some bonds have a *call feature*. When bonds are "callable" it means that the issuer can choose to retire the bond at any time. This will happen if the issuer can issue newer bonds with a lower coupon. Therefore, *call risk* is the possibility that the issuer will exercise a bond's call feature (if it has one). Whether or not a bond is callable or not is something that you should know about before you purchase it.

Sector risk is very similar to event risk. Certain firms experience business cycle downturns. Also, if investors started to hate bonds or have no reason to hold bonds of a certain type of company the bond's value can change. If you are an advocate of bonds and seek to load up, times like this can be exciting. With what you learn here, you will probably know exactly which bonds to buy or to avoid. With the exception of U.S. Treasuries, *default risk* is always a risk.

Liquidity risk is an obvious risk. Liquidity just means how fast a firm can come up with cash, or how quickly their assets can be converted to cash. That may be selling valuable assets or revenue churn, or not tying up cash flow into projects or too much inventory. Liquidity risk affects any debt instrument that is thinly traded (AKA low volumes). If there is not sufficient interest, and you want to sell, you may have to discount the price in order to entice buyers. Difficulty selling a bond in the secondary market is *marketability risk*.

Duration can also be a factor in risk assessment. The inverse relationship between price and yield is crucial to evaluating how the bond fits your objective. Estimating how sensitive a bond's price is to interest rate movements is unique to each bond. However, the best feature of bonds is that you always get paid no matter what. Just like a bank loan, the terms are set and the payments are fixed until the debt is retired.

All you really have to remember is that just because bonds are simple, you still have to consider those risk factors. Based on your specific goals for the investment some of these factors will be more relevant than others. Overall, reinvestment and event risk affect investors who hold the bonds until maturity. While interest rate, sector, and liquidity risk affect bond holders who sell before maturity.

ACTION ITEM

If you want to get all "Wall Street" there are several equations you can use to calculate a bonds risk. Since I don't want to annoy you, I won't explain how the "Macaulay's Duration" formula works. If you are upset about this, and are thinking this is important for you to know, then take a look at this mess.

$$D = \frac{\sum_{t=1}^{T}\dfrac{tC}{(1+r)^t} + \dfrac{TF}{(1+r)^T}}{\sum_{t=1}^{T}\dfrac{C}{(1+r)^t} + \dfrac{F}{(1+r)^T}}$$

(D - duration, C = Coupon, F - Face Value, T = Periods to Maturity, r = Periodic YTM, t = Coupon Received)

Just forget that you ever saw that. Instead, just remember the basics. Pay attention to interest rates. Don't ignore sector and financial events news because this will affect liquidity and marketability. Also, think about what you can invest in next before your bond matures. Really, those three things are the main things you need to know. Trying to quantify risk makes investors sleep better, but realistically those things are just best guesses. Just because something has a number attached to it does not make it solved.

By far the best risk management you can do is to do sound research and careful decision making that reflects your risk tolerance. In fact, that is all you can really rely on. Therefore, the next few chapters will explain the different types of bond issuers so you can make the right decisions that will fit your risk level and investment objectives, which is *all you need to sleep well* at night.

CORPORATE BONDS

Wasn't this covered in the bond fundamentals chapter? Bonds are boring and safe, who cares who issues the bonds, the terms are all that matters right? That is true, but the kind of bond you buy impacts the taxability of the investment, and overall investment quality. The issuer defines the type of bond. Knowing the expected terms for each the type of bond will give you more tools to assess which investment is right for you.

First some history, *bearer bonds* were used for post Civil War reconstruction (1865-1885). This bond was a negotiable instrument (like a check). Unlike modern bonds that are registered with the holder's name and address recorded on the bonds, these bonds did not have the name of the owner recorded on the bond or in the books of the issuer. A bearer bond belonged to whoever possessed it. A bearer bond was definitely more portable than gold, and could be just as valuable.

Due to the relative ease of transferring ownership, bearer bonds were used for large investments because it was easier to use than stacks of cash. Not only that, these bonds had interest coupons attached. So when the interest was due the bond holder clipped off the appropriate coupon and deposited it into a bank. Then at maturity the bond holder presented the bond certificate for redemption (repayment). Bearer bonds are archaic, and no longer issued, but were considered cutting edge at the time.

In the 1970's the bond market seriously evolved. Investors began to realize there was money to be made in trading bonds for a profit. Until then, the bond market was primarily a place for firms and governments to borrow money from pension funds and insurance companies. As computers evolved, the math became faster and finance professionals began to find creative ways to tap into the growing demand for bonds. By the 1980's junk bond traders were making billions.

As a retail investor, you can buy corporate, federal government, municipal, or sovereign debt just like anyone else. Each type of bond is similar, but has different characteristics. Therefore, this chapter will serve as your primer for corporate bonds. When people think of corporate debt they often focus on equity (stocks), but corporations rely far more heavily on bonds to finance their ongoing operations.

As mentioned earlier, a covenant is a set of restrictions that a bank will put on a loan. This usually entails supplying periodic financial statements, producing set levels of revenue, or not taking on any more debt. Bonds are easier than bank loans, there isn't a stringent covenant, and firms can set your own terms. Even the banks prefer this arrangement because they can charge fees to underwrite the bonds and also manage the payments with no credit exposure. It is also convenient for a firm to issue bonds, service the debt coupons, retire the debt at maturity, and then repeat as needed.

If Corporation X wants to build a new plant for $1 million it might be better for everyone to issue bonds to finance it. If the firm issues 1,000 bonds for $1,000.00 each it can build the plant. Maybe Corporation X has poor credit and must pay 15% for a 3 year bond. If the plant is expected to produce $1 million of extra revenue per year, this is a bargain. It may take a year to build the plant and get it running. However, if the revenue from a year two can retire the debt entirely, it is mutually beneficial for everyone.

Of course, every investment carries risk. Corporation X, (the issuer) may not be able to create the expected revenue, or the plant won't pass EPA standards, there may be cost overruns, or it may not function as expected. Maybe the products of Corporation X become obsolete, or they go out of business and default. Even if this happens there are some unique things about bonds that protect this investment.

Typically, a corporation must meet a specific level of earnings before it is permitted to issue additional bonds, this is referred to as the "earnings test." According to the Trust Indenture Act of 1939 and the Securities Act of 1933 (the *indentured* section). If the bond is *open ended* the issuing firm can issue additional bonds secured by the same assets as the original bond. If the bond issue is *closed ended* the issuer cannot issue additional bonds secured by the same claim on the same assets as the original issue (the support for the bond cannot be diluted).

Sometimes a corporation will issue *unsecured bonds* that have a "junior" claim on the assets. Bankers call this a *subordinate debenture*. In the case of default junior claims are subordinate to those of other bond holders. Hopefully, all of that legalese was not confusing. As mentioned previously, there are pre-established *liquidation rights* for publicly traded firms that work the same for everyone. All you have to remember is that if a firm were to go bankrupt or cease operations, this is the rank of payment when assets are liquidated to meet obligations:

1. Wages
2. Taxes
3. Secured creditors (can be bonds)
4. General creditors (including debenture)
5. Subordinate creditors (subordinate debentures)
6. Preferred stockholders
7. Common stockholders

Firms can also issue *commercial paper* which is short-term debt that matures in 270 days or less. This is a thriving market that banks and other large fiduciaries partake in daily. However, commercial paper is not a stock or a bond so it is exempt from the Securities Act of 1933. Since it is unregistered, the rules are set by the issuer and the counter party and standard securities regulations do not apply. This type of investment is usually reserved for large investors called *Qualified Institutional Buyers* (QIB).

Since commercial paper is usually only issued in $100,000.00 denominations, as a retail investor you will likely never deal with it. However, by knowing it exists helps you assess the strength or weakness of the corporate debt market. In fact, Standard and Poor's (S&P) have a commercial paper index that you can use to gauge the corporate debt market. Sometimes firms use commercial paper to build their credit rating so the next bond issuance will have a better rating and a lower coupon.

This is important to you because smart bond investors wait for events to occur that allow them to buy debt for cheap. If you can pay 0.50 cents for a $1.00 for debt from a firm that probably won't go out of business, you are being profitably contrarian. Overall, you should have enough information now to make some educated guesses about the pros and cons of this type of bond. Hopefully, this insight helps you find the right investment to suit your objectives.

ACTION ITEM

This action item will help you get acquainted with the corporate bond market. Corporate bonds can be investment grade or speculative grade (aka "junk" bonds). Take a look at some aggregate market activity info (finra-markets.morningstar.com/BondCenter/TRACEMarketA ggregateStats.jsp) so you can see how active the bond market is. Analyzing advances and declines as well as the most active investment grade and high yield bonds will help you assess the debt market. Consider this exercise as practice. A glance into market activity sometimes reveals corporate bonds that you may not have noticed before.

With anything investment you want to do some research. Look up bonds on the NYSE directory or on Barrons.com sometime during the day when the market is open. Watch the prices change. Then see which ones are the most popular and try to determine why. Watch the lower rate bonds for a moment, then watch the higher rated ones. Do you see any differences in volatility? You can also check out Moody's to find out the credit rating of the issuer.

In order to be listed on a public exchange, a publicly traded firm must release their audited financials. If you are very ambitious, go to the firm's website and look for "investor relations." Then just click the "SEC Filings" tab. The *8K* will be any announcements that could affect the financials, the *10Q* will be a quarterly filing, and the *10K* will be an annual filing.

Just like a banker, you can find out tons of information about the firm on the "tens." Reading those reports can also give you some investment ideas for their partner or vendor firms. For people who are socially conscious about what they invest in, municipal bonds might be a better investment than corporate debt, which is why those are covered next.

MUNICIPAL BONDS

If you are a socially conscious investor, or someone who is interested a tax free investment, municipal bonds may be a good fit for you. Since municipalities must operate on a budget, and due to the limits of taxation and fees, the list of infrastructure upgrades often goes unfunded. Unless some gracious benefactor makes a donation, cities usually tap the capital markets for funding by issuing *munis* (municipal bonds).

There are two different types of municipal bond structures. *General obligation* bonds are supported by sales tax or property tax. *Revenue bonds* are supported by the income derived directly from the project those financed. There are also *double barreled* bonds, which is a hybrid supported by creditworthiness and also project revenue. Unlike corporate bonds where $1,000.00 is the most common face value, munis are issued with a minimum denomination of $5,000.00.

Maybe an important bridge in your city is structurally unsound, and it will cost $20 million to repair it. Rather than waiting for the end of year taxes to come in, the municipality decides to issue 4,000 munis with a face value of $5,000.00 each. To make the offering competitive with other comparable bonds in the market the city decides to sell five year bonds with an annual coupon of 5%. Instead of increasing taxes the city uses the tolls to pay off the bonds. Since revenue from the project was used to pay the bonds those are revenue bonds.

As you can see, this is arrangement has a mutual benefit. The citizens get a new bridge without a major tax increase, while the investors get a decent return as well. If a municipality experiences a financial hardship, alternative terms are negotiated, but the bonds still get paid. Therefore, analyzing financial data and the feasibility of the proposed project is vital. If you are interested in this, there are several different types of revenue bonds available:

Airport bonds: Landing fees, fuel fees, and lease payments secure these bonds.

Industrial bonds: factories, industrial parks, and stadiums. Fees, concessions, and lease payments provide the backing.

Public power bonds: Pay for power plants. The sale of electricity provides the revenue.

Hospital bonds: Fund construction or renovation of a hospital equipment. Hospital revenue is used to pay the bonds.

Housing bonds: Pay for building single family or multifamily housing units. Mortgage payments secure the payments and the payments fund the bonds.

Transit bonds: Pay for public transportation projects, where the fares pay the bonds.

Water bonds: Finance water and sewer updates. Connection and usage fees provide the revenue to service the bond.

Highway bonds: Fund highways, and are funded by toll roads. Sometimes an increased "gas tax" or licensing fees secure bond payments.

There are also *municipal notes*, which is shorter term debt (like corporate commercial paper) with a maturity from 3 months to 3 years, the best quality being "MIG1" and "VMIG1." In some states there are also *special tax* bonds that are backed by excise taxes on cigarettes and alcohol or a special assessment on those who will benefit directly from the project.

Interest income from muni bonds is usually tax free at the federal level. At the state level, bonds purchased from your home state will usually be tax exempt, but bonds from outside of your state are subject to tax. It is also important to be aware that if you sell a muni before it matures and the price is more than your cost basis you are subject to *capital gains tax*.

Plus, the U.S. has parallel income tax systems.

Ordinary income tax, and *Alternative Minimum Tax* (AMT), which is a book of its own. In some situations, income from certain munis may be subject to AMT or *de minimus tax*, which is only paid on munis bought at a discount more than 0.25% (income tax and capital gains on the discount). It is boring to read, but *IRS Publication 550* is the definitive resource for researching investment income taxes.

With corporate bonds, the issuer produces a *prospectus,* which explains the investments details. With minis, a disclosure doc called an *official statement* is issued instead. In this document you would find out if the issuance would be a revenue or general obligation bond. Once that determination is discovered there are a few due diligence steps to do.

Depending on the municipality, general obligation bonds have less default risk than corporate bonds do. However, there are examples of cities defaulting on their obligations or the intended projects not working out as expected. For revenue bonds, as long as the revenue covers the investment it is a feasible project. Often there is less risk than general obligation bonds.

For any muni bond, you will want to analyze the economic health of the municipality. What a municipality collects in taxes is called the *Gross State Product* (GSP) Its tax burdens and the source of payments are important, but it is quite difficult to find out exactly what the taxes will be. However, by using the U.S. Census Bureau's (USCB) year to year data you can at least make some estimates.

You can use the USCB site (www.census.gov/govs/) to assess a city's existing debt, demographics fiscal history, budget, financial condition, unfunded pension liabilities, tax litigations, collection record, and also if property taxes are increasing or declining. You can also look up the *debt statements* to analyze direct debt, net direct debt, or overlapping debt.

Variable Rate Demand Obligations (VRDO) are debt instruments that allow issuers to receive short term financing rates when borrowing long term. VRDO's have a floating rate that can reset daily or weekly in correlation with demand. VRDO's provide yield curve diversity because short term rates are generally much lower than long term rates. For now, just learn how to compare munis to corporate bonds.

ACTION ITEM

Munis are often seen as a way to help local communities and can provide some tax relief for those in higher tax brackets with a civic agenda. This action item will show you how to compare a muni to a corporate bond. To find the *taxable equivalent yield* for Mr. Dweebus McMoney who is in a 28% bracket and wants to purchase a 9% muni at par, you would do the following:

FORMULA: Tax Exempt Yield/(100% - Tax Bracket)

ANSWER: 9%/(100% - 28%) = (9%/72%) = 12.50%
Mr. McMoney will need to earn 12.5% on a fully taxable instrument (like a corporate bond) to equal the tax free yield on a the 9% muni.

That example was pretty simple, and I am certain that you can see how this simple equation works. Without a doubt, you can easily re-perform it for Sally Denero who is in a 35% tax bracket. Here is the equation again. Do the quick math, and then check your answer with the correct one provided.

FORMULA: tax exempt yield/(100% - tax bracket)

ANSWER: 9%/(100%-35%) = (9%/65%) =13.85%
That same 9% muni is equivalent to a 13.85% fully taxable

instrument.

You can certainly see how a corporate bonds must have a higher yield to be equivalent to a muni. Since the corporate bond is taxable, the investor will realize a lower return (after tax). Obviously, the tax benefits of a muni can have a significant impact on an investor's returns. Here is how you can calculate the taxable yield on a corporate bond:

FORMULA: "Net yield" = taxable yield *(100%-tax bracket)

EXAMPLE: Net yield =12% *(100% -28%)
1. 12% *(100% -28%)
2. 12%*72% = 8.64%

ANSWER: The muni would need to yield 8.64% to be equivalent to the corp bond.

Now that you know how to research corporate bonds, you can now compare those to muni bonds. Bondview (www.bondview.com/research) can provide some insight into the muni market and MB.com shows recent trades of state bonds (in the bottom section). At Emma.msrb.org you can dig into the details of specific municipal bonds. The action item here may seem like too much work, but that work will literally pay off. If you don't like due diligence, maybe possibly government bonds will suit you better?

GOVERNMENT BONDS

As you can see, this book does not tell you exactly what to invest in. Instead, it gives you the knowledge and insight to figure out what is best for your specific objectives. Since everyone has their own agenda and goals the "best" investment will be different for everyone. Regardless of your preferences, if you have a managed portfolio it is 99% likely that you own some government bonds. Why?

This type of bond is a direct obligation of the government and considered the safest type of investment. Unlike all other bond or investment you can make, U.S. Treasuries have never defaulted. However, due to the low risk of this investment it won't be the highest yield, and usually just acts as a stabilizer for volatility in the rest of your portfolio. The three main types of U.S. Treasuries are, *Treasury Bills, Treasury Notes,* and *Treasury Bonds.*

T-Bills are short-term bonds that mature within one year or less from the time of issuance (with maturities of 4, 13, 26, and 52 weeks). T-Bills do not have a coupon, instead the investor is paid the difference between the purchase price and the par value (as interest). The one to six month T-Bills are auctioned off once a week, and the twelve month ones are auctioned off every four weeks. Due to the short maturities, and low risk, the yields available are usually quite low.

Treasury notes are issues with maturities of 1, 3, 5, 7, or 10 years and have a slightly higher yield than T-Bills. T-Note payments are made every six months until maturity. The difference between Treasury notes and Treasury bonds is length of maturity. T-Bonds are offered with maturities of 10, 20 and 30 years. The ten year treasury is by far the most widely followed because it is used as both a benchmark for the treasury market and also as a basis for the banks to calculate mortgage rates.

T-Bonds pay a semi-annual coupon (interest) and are issued quarterly by the U.S. Treasury in denomination that are multiples of $100.00. The initial price is determined by a public auction, and the interest rates are based on competing bonds. Bonds with higher coupons sell at a premium and those with lover ones sell at a discount. Typically, the longer the maturity date is the higher the yield will be.

T-Notes and T-Bonds pay a traditional coupon for interest, that pays every six months. At auction these bonds sell at a price that translates to a *yield to maturity* (YTM) or lower than that of the coupon. Both T-Notes and T-Bonds prices fluctuate so the yields remain linked to market prices. What happens if you have a 30 year bond with a 10% yield, and over the next few years, the rates fall and newer bonds are issued at 5%? Since investors can no longer buy the older 10% T-Bonds that bond's YTM will fall and its price will rise.

Generally, the longer the bond has to mature, the greater the price fluctuation will be. However, since T-Bills mature in such a short time there is very little price fluctuation. Even though there are not many differences between various U.S. Treasury products (T-Bills, T-Notes, T-Bonds) the differences explained are helpful to know when considering an investment and designing an investment plan. If you want to look these up, here is how you will read the data:

Rate	Maturity	Bid	Ask	Chg	Ask/yld
7 3/4	Feb. 01	105:12	105:14		5.50
5 3/8	Feb. 01	99:26	99:27		5.44

Column 1: Coupon rates
Column 2: Month and year of maturity
Column 3-4: Bid (Buy) and Ask (Sell)
Column 5: Price change from previous day
Column 6: YTM

NOTE: Bond's are quoted at a percentage of the par value. Government bonds are quoted in 1/32 increments of par while other bonds are quoted as 1/8.

Another US Treasury product worth knowing about is *Treasury Inflation Protected Securities* (TIPS). Unlike standard government bonds, TIPS provide protection against inflation. With TIPS the principal increases with inflation and decreases with deflation, which is measured using the Consumer Price Index (CPI). TIPS are available for 5, 10 and 30 year maturities, the coupon remains constant, and is paid semi-annually.

A $1,000.00 TIPS bond with a 2% coupon would receive $20.00. If inflation rises by 3%, the $1,000.00 principal is adjusted upward by 3% to $1,030.00. The coupon rate will still be 2%, but it is now applied to the new principal. So the new coupon payment is not $20.30 instead of $20.00. However, if the inflation rate fell by 3%, then the principal would now be $970.00, and the new coupon payment would then be $19.70 instead of $20.00.

Even though the investor won't realize those inflation adjustments until the bond reaches maturity, it is still considered taxable income. At any time before maturity the investor can sell the TIPS bond in the secondary market. TIPS bonds have an obvious advantage, but usually have a much lower interest rate than any corporate government bond. Like any other bond you should assess how well it fits with your investment goals.

The *Separate Trading of Registered Interest and Principal of Securities* (STRIPS) program allows investors to hold and trade the individual interest and principal components of T-Notes and T-Bonds as separate securities. STRIPS are essentially bonds that have the coupon removed and sold separately, but still pay the principal at maturity. STRIPS are created by financial institutions that purchase conventional treasury products and then create a separate

CUSIP to sell the coupon individually. Neither the coupon or the principal will receive any interest and is like a zero coupon bond.

   U.S. Savings Bonds offer a fixed rate of interest over a fixed rate of time, and savings bonds are not subject to state or local income taxes. These bonds are non-negotiable, but can't be cashed until at least six months after purchase. Savings bonds are like zero coupon bonds with interest that compounds semiannually, but is not paid until maturity or until it is redeemed.

ACTION ITEM

The main takeaway from this chapter is to introduce government bonds. This type of investment will definitely be part of your portfolio, but not something that you will focus your energy on. However, you may want to do some basic experimentation to assess what type of exposure you want for government bonds.

The New York Federal Reserve Bank's website provides a brief explanation of how to calculate the effective yield of a T-bill based on its price and the time until maturity. Also, *TreasuryDirect*, the website offered by the U.S. Treasury to enable investors to buy government bonds directly, explains how this process works.

The United States, Japan, and Europe have traditionally been the biggest issuers in the government bond market. If sovereign backed bonds are appealing to you, but you want something a bit more spicy. If so, *Government Sponsored Enterprises* (GSE) might be of some interest to you. A GSE is a privately owned company, but also a publicly chartered entity. There are five that issue "quasi" government *debentures*:

1. Federal National Mortgage Association (AKA Fannie Mae)
2. Federal Home Loan Mortgage Corporation (AKA Freddie Mac)
3. Federal Agriculture Mortgage Corporation

4. Federal Farm Credit Bank System
5. Federal Home Loan Mortgage Corporation. (AKA FHL Banks)

Privately owned firms that are supported by the government? Absolutely, Freddie and Fannie were created by Congress to buy consumer mortgages from the banks. They then bundle (securitize) those into *Mortgage Backed Securities* (MBS) to sell to investors on the secondary market. MBS function exactly like bonds. Both of these enigmatic products became well known in the brutal financial crisis of 2008-2009. Theoretically, MBS adds liquidity to the mortgage market by expanding the pool of funds available, which helps to lower rates.

Like MBS, Asset Backed Securities (ABS) are a bunch of similar loans bundled together and sold wholesale to one investor (like a pension fund) and each month the payments go to the investors just like any other bond arrangement. Except ABS bonds are created from auto, credit card, school loans, or other loan payments bundled and sold wholesale to investors. Like MBS, these loans can also be a *tranche* (portion of the investment) where lower quality and higher quality loans can be bundled into separate payouts. Depending on their stake, the individual investor's tranche determines who gets paid first.

As you can see, there are many options to you as an investor. The key is to learn a bit about each type of product/investment so you can figure out what will best fit your goals. Now that you know the basics about bond issuance, prices and maturity the material in the following chapters should help you make the best decisions you can. Just remember that no matter how much planning and research you do there is always risk.

BOND ISSUANCE
(PRIMARY MARKET)

Why is it important to know about how bonds are created? Frankly, it isn't a vital detail that will affect your portfolio. However, this information may be helpful if you own a mid to large size business and want to issue some bonds to fund a major project. To the average retail investor this part of investing is mostly invisible, so it may be interesting for you to learn "how the sauce is made."

The *primary market* refers to where debt instruments and securities are created. The *secondary market* refers to the exchanges where debt instruments and securities are traded. As a retail investor, you may never participate in the primary market, and exclusively operate in the secondary market. Understanding how the primary market operates may help you research what products are available, what those are used for, and what will fit your investment goals.

In the primary market for bonds, bankers originate underwriting for brokers and bank dealers by assisting states, local governments, school districts and also non-profit organizations with the issuance of debt instruments. This might include tax exempt and taxable municipal bonds, variable or fixed rate notes, or commercial paper (debt due in 270 days or less). Underwriting is a huge market, that exists globally.

To initiate any debt instrument issuance, a banker will start by analyzing the market and then communicates their financial institution's capabilities to the issuer. When the "mandate" (industry term for the type of deal/agreement) and "role" (industry term for the type of deal management) are determined, the deal proceeds. There are a variety of deal types available:

Riskless Principal: This means that one party is matched to another, and there is no residual inventory held.

Negotiated: Sometimes called a *private placement* where there is an exclusive agreement set up whereby they issuer agrees to an offering price for a select amount of *Qualified Institutional Buyers* (QIB).

Competitive Bid: This is where several bidders put forth their best price and terms, and the issuance is bought on an all or nothing deal basis.

Bought Deal: This is where an investment bank buys the entire issue from the issuer prior to formally marketing it to investors.

Backstop Deal: This is when an entity agrees to purchase

the unsubscribed (not bought) instruments, which provides security to the issuer that the entire issuance will be purchased.

As you can see, there is a variety of ways an investment bank can arrange an offering for entities that want to issue bonds. You can also see the appeal that debt issuance has over getting a bank loan. Why is the type of deal an investment bank creates important to you? The bank's mandate is key in deciphering the *issuance markup*, but the bank's role in deal can come in many forms:

<u>Sole Book Runner</u>: This agreement is where the main underwriter structures the deal and skims a profit from selling the issuance to the institutional public for more than they underwrote it for the issuer. Those institutional investors can retain or resell the issuance for a higher price.

<u>Joint Lead Manager</u>: This where the underwriting and execution of the issuance is shared by more than one bank. Typically, this occurs for a large offering and the lead managers split the profits.

<u>Co-Manager:</u> Multiple banks that participate in an offering are called a "syndicate." Syndicate members get a small piece of the offering profits, but don't have anything to do with the underwriting process.

<u>Agent</u>: This is when a banker or institution does not wish

to take ownership of the issuance, and just distributes the debt instrument on a "best effort" basis. Any unsold portion will be returned to the issuing firm.

Why does it matter what role a bank has in an issuance? As an investor, you may not ever be part of the *underwriting syndicate*, but you can still assess the due diligence done by what role the bank had in the deal. Some bankers would be offended by that statement, because *MSRB Rule G-32 and SEC Rule 15c2-12* explicitly states that underwriters are required to confirm the existence of a *continuing disclosure agreement*. There is an implied recommendation just by participating in the offering . However, depending on the type of deal, the level of *organic due diligence* will vary.

In fact, part of the due diligence is to acquire an *official statement* from the issuer, which outlines the specifics of the offering and provides internal details. For this document the issuer is expected to include financial statements, issue proceeds, and any material facts that could impact the issue if not disclosed. The underwriter will add this documentation to the *deal file*.

Deal structuring occurs when the issue is ready to be finalized and placed in the primary and secondary market. However, before that occurs a credit rating must be obtained from a credit agency (Moodys, S&P, Fitch). Once the rating is received the applicable documentation is retained in the deal file. Certain new issue documentation is required to be provided to co-managers and prospective investors through the *Municipal Securities Rulemaking Board's*

(MSRB) EMMA website.

In addition to this, an independent auditing firm will also complete a certification of the financials. Typically, the lead book runner will perform the due diligence process, which is usually completed prior to announcing the deal into the market. When the deal has been announced, a due diligence call is held prior to any settlements or finalization. The provisions in the bond's contract are also confirmed:

1. *Secured or unsecured debt (asset backed or not)*
2. *Senior or Subordinated debt (claims on assets)*
3. *Guarantee provisions (ability to pay)*
4. *Sinking fund provisions (buy back portions of the debt)*
5. *Debt maturity (date for principal payment)*

Once the deal is closed, the issuance is distributed to the co-managers and investors. *Settlement letters* must go out 60 days after the transaction closes and usually stored for several years. When the fees are paid the banker's move on to the next issuance deal and the investors decide what they want to do with the issuance.

If the investor chooses to sell it, they will do so in the secondary market. That market has both a *dealer* and an *auction* market. The dealer market consists of specialists who hold an inventory of securities or bonds and earns a profit by the price they pay and price they can sell (spread). The auction part involves a bid (selling price) and an ask (buying price) where one investor sells to another. The New York Stock Exchange (NYSE) is an example of an auction market.

Unless you are lucky enough or well connected, most of your investing will occur in the secondary market. However, I hope you can see how knowing how the issuance was created gives you an advantage over those that don't. In fact, watching what type of issuance is being traded and when will help you "follow the money" to find unique opportunities that other retail investors may not even notice.

ACTION ITEM

This chapter was designed to help you avoid one of the most common mistakes that investors make. Not buying bonds on the new issue market. With new issues you get the same price as everyone else. In fact, in the *retail priority* period you can buy municipal bonds before institutions can. Often retail investors ignore this or just don't think of it.

Investors often focus on yield only. The principal payment, the coupon, and the underlying business is important. Yet try to be mindful of the markups that exist in the secondary market. Too many investors just accept the price, but realistically the secondary market is a place for price negotiation. Knowing how the primary and secondary market fit together (in the next chapter), you will be able to observe the market better. As an investor primarily operating in the secondary market, this will give you an edge.

BOND TRADING AND SETTLEMENT (SECONDARY MARKET)

As mentioned earlier, in the capital markets, there is a *primary market* and a *secondary market*. As a retail investor, you may not have much access to the primary market. In fact, most of your activity will take place in the secondary market where securities or bonds are bought, sold, or traded. Just like stocks, bond prices move up and down for a variety of factors. With any investment you can "buy and hold" or look for arbitrage (buy low sell high) opportunities.

Just like stock/equity traders, there are also bond traders. However, you won't find any television shows with animated commentators trading quips about bond prices and yield curves. If you listen closely to the news you will hear these things, but most people ignore it. The people who know (what you now know) about bonds are often quiet. Realistically, if less people are interested in bonds, there will be less competition for the bargains.

Bond traders make money from buying or selling bonds to other market participants. Generally, the more bonds an issuer has outstanding, the more liquidity there will be for that bond to buy and sell it. Just like stocks, bonds with the most liquidity have closer spreads, which will often garner trading opportunities.

Bonds are negotiable instruments that can be transferred from one owner to another. The method of transfer depends on the form of ownership. A bond can be registered, or a book entry. A registered bond has the owner's name on it. To transfer a bond, the broker sends the bond to a transfer agent who reissues it in the name of the new owner.

Book entry bonds do not have certificates, instead a depository keeps records of ownership on its books for its members (the members are brokerages, banks other institutions) The members keep records, so transferring is just changing the records to reflect the trade. When two investors want to enter into a secondary market transaction they must agree not only to the price of the transaction, but on the exchange of the actual certificates and cash. The *settlement options* are as follows:

1. **Regular**: "T+2" Trade date plus 2 business days (The current policy of T+3 will be changing to T+2 very soon) so essentially three days.

2. **Cash Settlement**: Paying on the same day. Any transaction done before 2PM settles at 2:30. Anything after 2PM settles a 1/2 hour later.

3. **Sellers Option**: Can be 60 days after the trade date. This sometimes results in a lower price for the bond.

4. **Buyers Option:** Where the buyer sets the settlement date.

Bonds are usually quoted in multiples of $1,000.00, and prices are quoted as a percentage. A quote of 99 means that for every 1,000 of notional bond principal, you must pay $990.00. Upon settlement, accrued interest is owed to the seller as income for the time period they have held the bond. Since bonds pay semi-annually (depending on the bond), the proceeds of a bond trade can be calculated as follows:

(Price of the bond multiplied by notional) + accrued interest = Proceeds of the bond trade.

The main factors that affect bond prices are interest rates, credit quality, maturity, and liquidity (supply and demand). As mentioned before, bond prices go up when interest rates go down. (Newer bonds will have lower coupons, so bonds with higher coupons are more valuable). Also, as the price goes up, the yield will go down. Unfortunately, you cannot forecast economic data. However, you can take advantage of predictable pricing discrepancies.

Since bonds are a bunch of mini loans, the credit

quality of the issuer impacts the yield that investors will demand. The difference in yield is called the *credit spread*. The credit spread represents the creditworthiness of the issuer. This is calculated by comparing the issuer's bond to another of the same maturity. Poor quality issuers, and longer maturities will usually have a higher credit spread than higher quality and shorter maturities. The difference between long and short term yields is called the *term premium*.

Of course, supply and demand are constant factors in almost all marketplaces, but especially acute for capital markets. When new (or more) bonds are issued, the outstanding ones may fall in price in anticipation of the supply. Sector/industry new, competitive disadvantages, an expected credit downgrade, or a general deterioration of the issuers earnings will often have an effect on a bond's pricing. The same is true for good news, or a price spike in anticipation of a buy back (also called a "tender offer").

A *call provision,* which allows the issuer the option to buy back the bonds before maturity (when rates decline, they can issue new ones and pay less coupon out) firms with increasing revenue will often retire expensive debt by *refunding.* Of course, the investor receives the principal in full, accrued interest, and any future interest payments stop. Most often the bond holders are unable to reinvest their money into something with the same return.

Some bonds are *convertible* which means that under certain conditions, it can be exchanged for stock. If a convertible bond's conversion value is equal to the market price then a bond is trading at *parity*. Meaning that the market price, is higher than the market value of the stock the investor would receive upon conversion. Here is the basic equation for convertible bonds, and how this might work.

EXAMPLE:
$1,000.00 bond
$50.00 agreed upon "conversion price"
$60.00 cost per share in the market

1. *Par value of bond/conversion price = conversion ratio*
1,000.00 divided by $50.00 = 20 shares

2. *Parity price of the bond = conversion value (number of shares* price per share)*
20 shares at $60.00 each = $1,200.00

Profiting from price disparity and differentials of the same or similar security is called *arbitrage*. Anytime the market price of the convertible bond does not reflect the value of the common stocks that would be received (if the bond were converted into stock) the bond would be selling at a *discount to parity* or the stock might be selling at a *premium to parity*. Arbitrageurs could use this to profit on a trade.

EXAMPLE:
A convertible bond X is trading at $1,350.00 in the market. Each convertible bond can be converted into 40 shares. When the trader looks up the stock, they discover it is trading at $35.00 per share. What can they do? Let's walk through steps 1-3:

1. *Par value of bond/conversion price = conversion ratio*
$1,350 divided by 40 = $33.75 per share
$33.75 is the cost of 40 shares
(The stock is trading at $35.00 in the market)
The *conversion ratio* is $1,350.00

2. *Parity price of the bond = conversion value (number of shares* price per share)*
$35.00 multiplied by 40 shares = $1,400.00
The *conversion parity* is $1,400.00

3. *Profit = Conversion parity minus conversion ratio*
$1,400.00 minus $1,350.00 = $50.00 *profit* for each convertible bond that you can buy.

Based on that analysis, an arbitrageur would buy the bond at $1,350.00 and convert it to stock for $1,400.00 and make a profit of $50.00 per bond. Obviously, this profit would exist until the bond price increased to at least $1,400.00 and other savvy people would notice this pricing disparity as well. However, as you can see if you know how bonds work, and everyone else is focused on stocks, you can search for market discrepancies.

It can be difficult at times to choose between two bonds of the same class. Interest rates on non-treasury securities is called the *spread* or the *risk premium.* To analyze the yield spread between the difference between two bonds can be measured on a relative basis by taking the ratio of the yield spread to yield level. *(Yield on Bond A minus the yield on Bond B) divided by the yield on Bond B).* You can also compare two bonds by a *yield ratio*. (*Yield on Bond A divided by the yield on Bond B*).

One of the most common ways to profit from buying and selling bonds is to look for bargains. If a firm has a few bad quarters or an event (like executive fraud) the ratings agencies will often downgrade the issuer's credit rating from investment grade to junk. It does not mean that the bond will default, or that the firm is going bankrupt. Usually, the firms have significant cash flow to support the coupon. However, since most large pension funds and insurance companies are not allowed to hold anything other than investment grade bonds event risk bonds go on sale.

To trade on the open market (NYSE, etc) a firm must meet certain requirements or its stock is put on the *pink sheets* and sold on the *over the counter market* (OTC) instead of the exchanges. The *yellow sheets* are the same thing, but for bonds. The yellow sheet bid and ask quotations are published weekly by the national quotation bureau. Trading activity for NYSE and AMEX listed bonds appears each day in the newspaper. If you are feeling really ambitious check that out. However, be mindful that the OTC market is not transparent like other secondary markets. So be careful buying or selling the OTC.

ACTION ITEM

The purpose of this chapter is not to convince you to become a bond trader or to evangelize market speculation. The content here should provide a context for how the secondary market operates. As a retail investor, you won't have the tools to trade individual bonds (Bloomberg maintenance fees are $14,000.00 a month per terminal). Plus, with markup and fees, trading individual bonds may be cost prohibitive. However, this action item should help you use some basic strategies to do some trading without having a Bloomberg terminal.

I don't recommend buying and holding *Exchange Traded Fund*s (ETF). However, you can do arbitrage with bond ETFs and bond funds. An ETF is a basket of stocks or bonds traded under one ticker. If you were to buy the ticker BSJJ, you would be buying a variety of high yield corporate bonds set to mature in 2019. Or JNK, which is a basket of low quality, high yielding bonds from a variety of sources. If it is traded on a public exchange there are strict rules for disclosure and transparency. To research the holdings, you just pull up the ticker and then look at what is in the ETF.

I could certainly create an entire book about how to research bonds, and ETFs. However, this book is designed to be a primer, and is certainly complex enough already. Overall, this book was made to help the average investor discover more about bonds and implement bonds into their overall strategy. Since everyone has different goals and investing agendas, this book should provide you with a good enough foundation to make some educated choices. Now go do some internet research on a few ETFs from this list of bond ETFs. Also, if you need to go investigate your broker.

YIELD CURVE

The *yield curve* is important to bonds, but usually the reason why people think bonds are boring. Stocks are unpredictable, which makes those exciting. Bonds are stable, and generally adhere to economic theory, two things that most people find annoying. Why should you even care about a yield curve? Rate changes affect financing costs, which affect financing costs, which affect expenditure decisions. The slope of the curve is what bond holders use to predict rising or falling rates.

Based on what you have learned so far, do you know why the yield curve is important to bond investing? After this chapter you will know plenty about how to use this tool. If you have never seen a yield curve before, it is a graph that plots time from shortest to longest maturity date on the horizontal axis, and the lowest to highest yield on the vertical axis. Based on those two data points the curve shows the relationship between yield and maturity.

By comparing similar bonds with differing maturities you can generate a graph that will show how yields will change as the maturity lengthens. A yield curve takes three basic shapes, *normal*, *inverted*, and *flat*. The normal yield curve is positive sloped and depicts "usual" market conditions where the yield increases as maturities lengthen. The typical yield curve would show lower yields in the shorter maturities and higher yield in longer maturities. Here is an example of a "normal" yield curve.

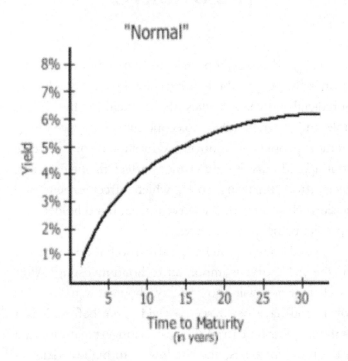

Under normal conditions The yield (coupon) percentage goes up as the maturity increases because an investor wants more interest to tie up their money for a longer period of time. If short term yields are higher than long term yields, the curve slopes downward. This type of curve is called an *inverted curve* or *negative curve*. In this environment, yields are highest for short term maturities and decrease when maturity increases. This kind of curve often precedes a recession. Here is an example of an inverted curve.

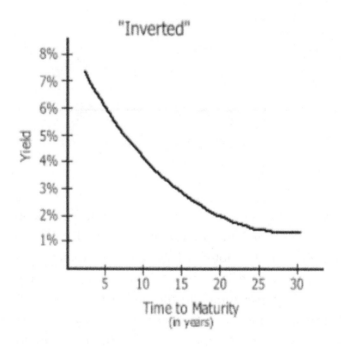

A *flat yield curve* is when there is little or no variation between short and long term yields. It also implies, that demand and supply are similar across all yields and maturities

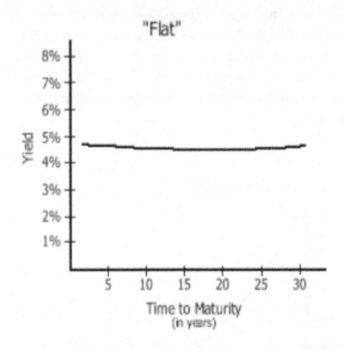

"Flat"

When the curve is *positive sloped* (normal) investors desire a higher rate of return for taking on risk for a longer period of time. Economists believe that a steeper curve means that investors expect strong future economic growth with higher future inflation (higher interest rates). A negative sloping curve (inverted) means that investors expect a sluggish economic growth with lower future inflation (lower interest rates). A flat curve indicates that investors are unsure about future economic growth and inflation.

Again, why does this matter and why should you care about yield curves? Depending on the economy, the shape of the curve changes. Investors who are able to predict how rates will change can invest accordingly. The shape of the yield curve also affects stocks and also your purchasing power. Investors make decisions based on what they think will happen in the future. If everyone expects the future rates to be higher and you can see this on a yield curve, you know that longer term bonds will have a better return. The transverse is true for the investor sentiment seen on an inverted curve.

It is also important to realize that *real interest rates* are what investors in fixed income securities actually receive once inflation is taken into account. If a 10 year investment yields 7% and inflation is 3% for that time period, then the real interest rate is 4%. Realistically, there is no way to predict inflation. Overall, bonds will provide your stock portfolio some balance. However, if you are investing it is best to know what to buy and when to sell, and when to do so.

ACTION ITEM

The yield curve is important for bond investors. Yet, as a retail investor you may not have the trading tools that bankers do. Even if you have access to those tools, it is quite difficult to speculate. For big banks, government bonds have become a useful tool swap trade hedging. As a retail investor, this will likely never be something that you will ever do.

The term *convexity* is a measure of the relationship of a specific bond to the yield curve, which demonstrates the interest rate changes during the duration of the bond. You can get quite technical with bonds, or just be aware of the market and basic yield curve theory. Evaluating your bond portfolio based on the yield curve is helpful, but not the only tool you should use.

Since other bonds will be based on the interest rate, it never hurts to look at a dynamic yield curve or stochastic indicators for the 30, 20, 10 or the 5 year yields to get some insight into the market sentiment. Whether you are adding more bonds to your portfolio or selling, the yield curve slope can help influence your decision making. With this knowledge you can make more objective long term decisions.

CALCULATING COUPONS

Now that you know what to expect with the different types of debt instrument investments, knowing the finer details of how you get paid is key. Just in case you forgot, the *coupon* is the term used for the interest on the loan you are giving to the bond issuer. The stated rate of interest that the issuer promises to pay the bondholder is called the *nominal yield*.

With a 10% coupon (unheard of but makes the numbers easier), the bondholder receives $100.00 per year for each $1,000.00 of par value (10%*1000). The $100.00 of interest will be paid in two $50.00 semiannual payments. Nominal rates don't change, but market prices can fluctuate greatly. *Current yield* measures the interest that the investor receives from the bond compared to its current market price. This is calculated by dividing the annual interest by the bond's current yield.

Current yield = Annual Interest Payment / Current Market Price

EXAMPLE:

10% bonds purchased at $800 would have a current yield of 12.5%

($100 yearly interest/$800 market price)

Therefore, an investor pays $800 for a bond with 10% coupon and earns 12.5% interest

The current yield is used to make an assessment on the relationship between the current price of a bond and the annual interest generated. The current yield is the actual yield that the investor would get. However, using current yield as the rate of return does not take into consideration the price appreciation on a discount bond, or the price depreciation on a premium bond when held to maturity.

The *yield to maturity* (YTM) is the anticipated return associated with the bond and is also the yield quote done in the marketplace. That may seem confusing, so explaining this in another way will help. The current rate (annual interest/current price on the bond) is the return the investor gets if they were to purchase the bond right now. YTM is the yield one can expect if they hold the bond to maturity.

As a reminder, when interest rates rise the value (price) of existing bonds will usually decline since the demand for existing bonds that now offer lower interest will decline. Thus, driving down prices. If interest rates decline, the value (price) of the existing bond will increase because those are now worth more than a new bond with a lower coupon rate. Therefore, yield and coupon rates have an inverse relationship. All you have to do is remember this general rule:

Interest rates increase = Price of existing bond decreases
Interest rates decline = Price of existing bond increases

Due to this fact, there will always be *discount, premium,* and *par* bonds. All of which have advantages and disadvantages. However, unlike stocks a bond almost always repays the investor (unless the issuer defaults) and the coupon is fixed. I think these terms are well understood by now, and this concept was covered earlier. However, I will still provide some example calculations so you have a model to use.

DISCOUNT BOND: (Price decrease = Yield increase)

If the interest rates rise, new bonds will be issued with coupon rates higher than 10%. Investors are now able to earn more than 10% nominal yield printed on the bond. The price of the bond must be reduced to make its yield competitive with the newer higher yielding bonds. Thus, the increase causes the 10% bond to sell at a discount to par value.

10% bond is purchased at the price of 90 (90% of $1,000.00 face value)

Nominal yield is still 10% since the issuance does not change. The current yield is now 11.11%, which is greater than the nominal yield. The annual interest is the same ($100.00) but the cost of the bond is now $900.00.

($100.00 annual interest payment/$900.00 market price = 11.11% current yield)

If held to maturity, the bond will pay $1,000.00, which is $100.00 more than its purchase price. This additional $100.00 in capital appreciation adds to the bond's overall rate of return. Thus, the yield to maturity (11.72%) will be more than the current rate of 11.11%

PREMIUM BOND (Price increase = Yield decrease)

If the rates decline the new bonds will be lower than 10% making the 10% bonds more valuable because investors will pay more for a bond with higher interest. Here is a typical example.

A 10% bond is purchased for $110.00 (110% of $1000.00 face value)

The nominal yield is still 10%, the current yield is less than the nominal yield. The interest payment is still $100, but the cost is now $1,100.00. The current yield is now 9.10%. Why?

$100.00 (annual interest) payment received divided by $1,100.00 (current market price) = 9.10% current yield.

If the bond is held to maturity, the owner will receive $1,000.00 This is $100.00 less than the bond's purchase price. While the yield is 9.10% the yield to market (YTM) will be less to reflect the premium that is lost over the life of the bond. (8.50% less than the current yield of 9.10%). Even for professionals, using an online calculator to calculate YTM is best practice.

PAR BOND (Equal)

Nominal yield of 10%, current yield equals the annual interest payment (100.00 in two 50 semiannual payments), purchased at par it will be redeemed at par at maturity, the YTM will also be 10%. So if a 10% bond selling at par ($1,000.00) the nominal yield and current yield, and YTM are all equal for a bond at par.

As mentioned earlier, the "par value" of a bond is the amount that the issuer agrees to pay the investor when the bond matures. This is also called the "principal" or "face value." An investor that buys a bond with a par value of $1,000.00 can expect to receive $1,000.00 upon redemption. $1,000.00 is a common par value for corporate bonds, and $5,000.00 is common for munis.

The par value can actually differ from the market value (i.e. the price and investor pays to purchase the bond). Most bonds are sold at par value, but can be bought or sold below or above par value. A bond sold for less than par is selling at a discount, while a bond that is sold for more is selling at a premium. For yields, there are a couple of handy calculations that are relatively simple to do:

Current Yield = Annual coupon divided by the current price of the bond.

Capital Gains Yield = Expected change in bond's price divided by beginning year price.

Calculating the current rate, the yield to maturity, and a coupon should be something that you can do on your own or with an online tool. Overall, bonds will be reliable and there won't be crazy volatility in the market. The main goal of the entire *Smart Money* series is self-empowerment, which is why this was covered with greater detail. Hopefully, this chapter will further enable you to make investment decisions that fit your needs and objectives.

ACTION ITEM

As someone with finance industry experience I have different perspective on investing. The average retail investor just wants the basics. For the most part you know almost everything about how bonds work. However, if you want to be a complete finance nerd like I am, then learning how to compute the amount of a discount will be interesting. If not, skip this action item and don't bother learning about this.

Remember Treasury Bills (T-Bills) from the government bonds chapter? T-Bills have a year or less to maturity at the time it is issued and have no coupon. Instead T-Bills are sold at a "discount from par value." Essentially, the owner earns interest when the bills mature at par. (Sold for more than the purchase price) T-Bills are traded at a "discount yield" which determines the amount of discount and the price of the bill. If you are given the discount yield, you can compute the amount of the discount like this:

Discount = (Days to maturity/360)*rate (Percentage - Discount yield)

(Per $100.00 of maturity value)

Price ($) - $100.00 - discount (per $100.00 of maturity value)
Dealers use 360 days a year

T-Bill due in 147 days and trades on a 5.32% discount yield basis.

First, find the discount rate

$D + (M/360) * R(\%)$

$=(147/360)*(.0532)$

$=2.1723$ *full discount*

Thus, the investment receives a discount of 2.1723 per $100.00 of maturity value. For a $100,000.00 bill the discount is $2,172.30 (2.1723 multiplied by 1,000) now calculate the price:

$P = \$100.00 - D$

$= \$100.00 - 2.1723$ *(per $100.00)*

$P = 97.8277$

The dollar price of the T-Bill is equal to $97,8277 for every $100.00 for face (or maturity) value. So $100,000.00 sold on a 5.32 basis would cost $97,827.70 and mature after 147 days. If you want to be a total nerd you can also do this equation for the bid and the ask to see the spread cost.

COMPOUNDING

Of course, you can always look for discounted opportunities or seek out arbitrage situations. However, the best part about bonds is that you can make money from literally doing nothing. That nothing is called *compounding*. Here is the compounding formula, even without chalkboard, at any angle this looks intimidating right?

Compounded growth = Amount Invested multiplied by (1+i)N
N= Number of compounding periods
i = Percentage of interest paid

EXAMPLE:

10 year bond
20 compounding periods (Bond pays interest twice a year)
e.g N=20

The percentage paid in interest is half of the compounding rate 7% interest/2 = 3.5% e.g.   I = 3.5%

Invest 25,000.00

$$25{,}000*(1+.035)*20 = \$49{,}744.72$$

If you don't have a financial calculator, to raise 1.035 to the 20th power you must multiply it times itself twenty times before multiplying it by 25,000.00. Which is somehow easier? Unfortunately, this kind of needless complexity is what drives people away from investing. People attracted to bonds want simplicity, and equations often make things more complicated than necessary.

Instead, try looking at this from a reasonable perspective that you can actually use. Compounding just means that you reinvest any money you make on your investment back into your original investment. Compounding can be done with anything that generates a constant stream of income. Instead of messing around, I suggest you go to an online compounding calculator and do some experimentation with those same numbers, which will take less than a minute.

The main factor to remember with compounding is that the longer you let it automatically occur, the more money you will have. This is why the secure returns of bonds are excellent. Since you know what your return will be, and when you will get paid back you can calculate what type of return you need to achieve your goals. I suggest using the compounding calculator to do some experiments. I guarantee that you with only a few trials, you will figure out the rate you need to achieve your goals. The nice thing about bonds is that you get paid no matter what.

ACTION ITEM

Someone attracted to bonds is interested in small, but secured gains. Billy Beane, the Oakland A's baseball manager that Michael Lewis made famous in his book *Money Ball* used *sabermetrics* to determine the most effective singles hitters. Why? If you have not read this fantastic book, Beane had the lowest payroll. Due to that, he could not afford big name home run sluggers. However, barely viable veterans who could reliably hit singles were cheap.

His strategy was that bunch of singles equals the bases loaded, which is consistent runs scored, which equals wins. That philosophy is the bond portfolio. Therefore, this action item is simple, visit any online compounding calculator and do some experiments of your own. What I want you will discover is how the longer you let compounding automatically occur, the more money you will have. This experiment should help inspire you to stop waiting to invest.

PORTFOLIO STRATEGY

Most people don't hold bonds exclusively. However, there are some savvy investors who look for deals and make a fortune. There are others who exclusively buy and sell bonds in the secondary market for profit. The average investor will not do either of those things. Instead, they will have bonds in their portfolio to offset stock losses.

Based on what you learned in this book so far you should be able to find the right kind of bonds to suit your financial goals. Whatever you decide to do, here is a quick equation that most people use to evaluate investments:

Divide 72 by the Yield to Maturity (YTM) = This is the time it will take to double your money.

How long will a 5% return (every year) take to double your money?

ANSWER: 72/5 = 14.4

14 years and 4 months.

That is nice to know, but the most important part to remember is that about bonds move in the opposite direction of interest rates. When rates rise, bonds fall and vice versa. If you buy a bond and hold it until it matures, swings in interest rates and the resulting swings in the bond's price won't matter. But if you sell your bond before it matures, the price it fetches will be largely related to the interest rate environment. Yet bonds are still predictable. Essentially, there are passive and active strategies.

Passive strategy entails buying and holding bonds until maturity, or investing in portfolios that track bond indexes. Passive approaches suit investors that look for capital preservation, income diversification, and have no desire to capitalize on arbitrage or trading. The interest rate environment affects the prices buy-and-hold investors pay for bonds when they first invest and again when they need to reinvest their money at maturity.

The laziest passive strategy is to invest in a bond fund that benchmarks (gets the same return) against a popular index. With bond funds, portfolio managers change the composition of their portfolios if and when the corresponding indexes change, but they do not generally make independent decisions on buying and selling bonds. For more strategic investors, laddering, the barbell, and the bullet are often used.

A *laddered* bond portfolio entails buying bonds with different maturities and reinvesting the ones that mature into new ones. Due to the fact that no two bonds mature at the same time, you can create a diversified maturity distribution. You might have a two, three, and four year bond, then when one bond matures, depending on which rates are better, you can reinvest the proceeds into the next rung, or a longer term one. If the rates are rising, reinvesting in another bond works well, and if the rates are falling, you can rely on the extra interest from the rolling bonds. This strategy is often likened to *dollar cost averaging* with stocks and decreases reinvestment risk.

Laddering is a popular strategy for people who want to invest for long term objectives. This strategy is appealing for someone saving for a child's future education, or a retiree who seeks a predictable income stream. The downfall of this strategy is that the investment is committed for a long period of time and if the bond is not guaranteed (only US treasury bonds are guaranteed), this can be problematic. The periodic return of the principal does give the ladder investor some flexibility and protection from interest rate volatility due to the spread of coupons and maturities.

Another popular strategy to use with bonds is called the *barbell*. With this strategy, you only invest in short term and long term bonds. Having some of your principal maturing early, and some later, gives you more flexibility to invest elsewhere (if there is an opportunity) and still receive payments. If rates rise, the short term bonds can be held to maturity, and then just reinvested into the long term bonds with higher yields. The barbell strategy will give you more liquidity and allows you to respond to emergencies quicker.

The *bullet* is investing at different times into bonds that all have the same maturity date. This strategy is used when you are saving for a big purchase to be made at a specific time. The variety of bonds in this portfolio reduces interest rate risk, and is less likely to lose value when rates change. This is a good approach if rates are expected to change frequently and the amount you want to invest is unpredictable. These strategies will enhance your yield, yet there are times when you might want to sell a bond before its maturity.

Active strategies try to outperform bond indexes by buying or selling bonds to capitalize on price movements. This type of investor enjoys the benefits of bonds, but must make some strategic decisions about the economy, the direction of interest rates and/or the credit environment at the right time. One traditional technique is to do split investing with zeroes.

Zero coupon bonds do not pay interest at regular intervals. There are no coupons, hence the name. Instead the investor purchases the bond at a deep discount from par value. Usually, the longer the period until the bond matures, the deeper the discount. This type of bond is redeemed for its full value when it matures. The difference between the purchase price and the amount the investor receives when the bond matures is interest.

Why buy this? Investors who desire a lump sum payment at some future date will find this arrangement appealing. Let's say you need $20K in 2018 to pay for a child's first year of college. In 2000 you bought a zero with the par value of 20K. This was scheduled to mature in 2018. You paid 5K for the bonds, and you won't receive interest payment until the bonds mature in 2018, when you will receive 20K.

The yields on zeroes are usually slightly lower than those on comparable interest bearing bonds. However, the prices of zeroes are more volatile, so selling early might result in losing a significant amount of the principal. Split investing with zeroes would be with $100,000.00 to invest, $50,000.00 would go to buy *zeroes* that might double in value. Then the other $50,000.00 is invested into riskier bonds with higher yields.

Total return investing probably the most widely used active investing approach. An investor seeks out undervalued bonds, holds those until the price rises, then sells before maturity to realize a profit. This strategy the same as buy low and sell high opportunities of arbitrage. Looking for bonds where the credit worthiness of the issuer is rising or an underperforming firm has implemented new/better management.

The active investor may also look for depressed bonds that may rise in price due to economic conditions, interest rate changes, or some global growth pattern or event. Due to the natural business sector rotation that occurs in the market, there is usually an opportunity to do this with underperforming sectors. Then to sell those bonds and realize capital gains when the economic cycle turns. Then buy into another.

Shortening or lengthening the duration based on yield curve projections is another way the active investor can capitalize on price movements. When short term interest rates are lower than longer term rates ("normal" curve) a bonds yield is lowered and the price rises as it gets closer to maturity. Selling certain bonds for profit at that time occurs often. If the active investor has a variety of low and high quality bonds, there are more options for capitalizing on price movements and opportunities for arbitrage.

Neither active or passive investing is better. The bond market is quite efficient, and bond investors think more like bankers than gamblers. There are ways to beat benchmarks, but before you attempt to do so, you must do plenty of economic research and calculations. Like any other information, you can make several decisions with it. Always try to make the one that best fits your financial goals. If that means being passive, then there is no shame in that.

ACTION ITEM

For the most part your portfolio can be anything you want it to be. It should suit your needs and fit your goals, which might not be a cookie cutter match of your neighbor's bond portfolio. Overall, there are five steps you need to take:

1. Set investment objectives (goals)
2. Establish an investment policy (allocation guidelines)
3. Set your strategy (active or passive)
4. Select your assets (types of bonds)
5. Measure and evaluate the performance (select and use a benchmark - like a bond index)

Even if you have someone manage your portfolio for you, those five steps are the key to your success. Having a reason to invest also makes it easier, and will give you a purpose focused mindset. Whatever portfolio ideas in this chapter that fit your objective can be implemented to suit your personal comfort level and investment objective. The action item for this chapter is for you to create a goal, then use some of those ideas to build a structure around your investment goals and milestones.

HOW TO DO SYNTHETIC SWAPS

Unbeknownst to people who don't work in financial services, *swaps* are big business. Unless you are involved in corporate finance or get excited about auditing this chapter won't be that useful to you. In fact, if you want, you can just skip to the action item at the end. However, if you want to find out how Corporate America makes it easier for you to buy and sell bonds, then read on.

What if you could get a yield increase or get better capital gains or improve your tax exposure would you do it? Maybe you just want to upgrade quality, or increase your yield to maturity? Maybe you need to diversify or hedge some market holdings? It could be that you need to adjust to some state law changes? Whatever the reason large firms with international exposure use swaps everyday.

Large corporations worry, and have millions of dollars at stake, so paying a premium to lock in a fixed profit is like writing off insurance expenses. In fact, as a retail investor, you may never encounter swaps, and I doubt you will ever have any need for this product. Plus, knowing about this will help you conceptualize the vastness of a part of the bond market that most people don't even know exists.

A swap is a derivative contract through which two parties exchange a financial instrument of some type. No principal is ever exchanged. Usually, one cash flow is fixed and one is variable (based on a floating rate or benchmark). An interest rate swap (the most common) is the same for both sides of a currency. WTF? Here is a fictitious example, that might inspire you to be creative with your own bond portfolio.

Company X is in California in the USA, and company Z is in Manchester England. For whatever reason company X needs to pay something in British pounds, and company Z needs to pay something in US dollars. Since each firm has indigenous benefits in its own country, these companies can create a swap agreement. Since currency rates change daily, firms who have significant stakes in overseas trade will do this to lock in a fixed rate. Swaps are usually not a retail investor product.

The reason why swaps are being mentioned is so you are aware of how important and liquid the bond market is. Swaps may sound impressive, but after working in a bank for several years I see it a bit differently. Bond investors believe that they are getting a yield pickup when swapping. However, as you know by now, the trap with this thinking is that most often when interest rates rise, and bond's price falls.

Imagine a 6.25% YTM, but now similar bonds have a 7.5% YTM. Why not decide to sell the old bonds and buy the new ones to make 1.25%. More interest is exciting right? Actually, it isn't. Why? The bond you already own will have gone down in value as interest rates rose. Therefore, you will have less money to reinvest into the new bond. The YTM will be higher, but you will have less money earning that interest.

Technically, this investment return (dollars earned) will probably be about the same from either bond. Yet, since the firm who did this had to pay the broker dealer a fee to buy and sell the new bond, the new bond might be a lower return. As retail investor this is completely useless. Yet if you are a business person and interested in getting more involved in the swap market you might be wondering how you can even tell if a swap is a good idea? If you need to lock in a fixed profit swaps work great.

If you want to crunch some numbers I will provide an example. Once again I will use 10%, which is an unlikely rate, but it makes the math is easier.

EXAMPLE:

Maybe you have to swap into a lower yield bond from a higher one so you can earn a higher return when you sell it again. What? Why? How?

1. You have $20,000.00 invested that matures in 5 years with a 10% coupon.

2. This provides $2,000.00 a year in income. (2,000*0.10) in two payments a year.

3. This will pay $10,000.00 in interest over the remaining life of the bond, but you can sell the bond for $25,000.00 and reinvest in a 5 year bond with an 8.25% coupon. (Lower interest, but a profit on the sale)

4. Your original bond provides $10,000.00 over the life of the bond (2,000*5)

5. The new bond will be for $25,000.00 with a coupon of 8.25% coupon. (lower interest, but more)

6. The annual income from the 8.25% coupon is 2,062.50 a year (25,000*0.085)

7. This equals $10,312.50 over the life of bond

8. $10,312.50 - $10,000.00 = $312.50 better

9. 20,000 bond sold for 25,000 = $5,000 better

10. If your tax rate is 25% and you pay $1250.00 in taxes on the $5,000 capital gain from selling your bond (25,000-20,000) you only make $9,062.50 versus the $10,000.00 if you remained reinvested in the original one. Even if you add the $312.50 you still would have done better without doing a swap.

11. Once you add commission (2-3%) this swap looks even worse.

This example is a way to show you how swaps work. Banks make a ton of loot for not doing anything except maintaining a network, investor correspondence, matching counter parties, and booking trades for a fee. As a retail investor, this example might spark some creativity, and show you how to analyze a swap. Honestly, you could have skipped this chapter, but if you read this far the action item will be a significant reward.

ACTION ITEM

If you kept reading or you just skipped down to the action item, this technique is a unique idea that you can use anytime you need to. The purpose of this chapter was to inspire you. Even if you didn't discover what swaps are I will explain a *synthetic swap* in a super simple way without any math at all. After you learn this try to think of your own ways to tweak the market with swapping.

It is sometimes a good idea to take a strategic loss for tax purposes. If you are familiar with stocks you know what a *wash sale* is. If not, it just means that you cannot sell and buy back the same security for 30 days before or after the trade date if there is a loss. With bonds this regulation does not apply, so technically you can claim a loss and stay invested where ever you want to be.

As you know, for bonds there are three things that identify it, issuer (who owes you) coupon (interest received) maturity (time until it is paid). For a bond to be determined a substantially different security, you only have to change two of the three things. Sell HP and buy IBM, or sell Ford and buy GM and add a few dollars difference.

Technically, you are just buying a replacement bond with the same characteristics of the original one, staying invested, but still able to take the tax loss. If you need to, read the last sentence again. If you need to take a tax loss, you can just swap one bond for another without a significant impact on your portfolio. Now, try to think of a few ways that you can do other synthetic swaps that might fit your investment objectives.

RESEARCHING A BOND

This chapter was written for the more advanced investor. Granted the information will be worthwhile, but it is more complex. Researching equities or debt is a blend of both art and science. There are numerous techniques, and just as many opinions. What I will explain here will be very basic to some and too complex for others. I could easily write a 300 page book on this aspect of investing.

However, this is not that book. The purpose of the *Smart Money* series is to empower investors, and promote economic equality for everyone. Like the rest of the books in this series, this book will give you enough knowledge to feel confident about your investment choices and allow you to know exactly what to research about the topics that fit your lifestyle the best. Therefore, leaving this information out would make the book incomplete.

Something important to realize about bonds and debt is the *time value of money*. This just means that the money you have today will have a different amount of purchasing power in the future, which is typically less. Therefore, it is important to think about your investments in this way. Professionals calculate this into the yield. As a retail investor, you may not want to add this detail, but it is still a good thing to be aware of.

Bonds can provide many functions for a diversified portfolio, but most often bonds function as a stable yield that will support the volatility of a diversified stock portfolio. Since the inflation rate is unpredictable, calculating the present or future value of any cash flow is merely proforma (speculative forecasting). Analysts use the following formula to do so.

$$PV = \frac{C}{(1 + i)^n}$$

This equation and diagram is great, but not very useful for the average investor. Overall, you can think about a bond's payout in a couple of ways. What will the payout's purchasing power be in the future? What will that payout be worth now? This may seem confusing, but really both of those analysis tactics will result in the same decision. Here is a PV diagram.

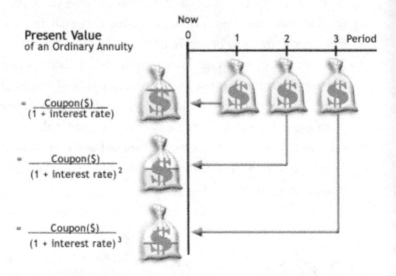

Present Value
of an Ordinary Annuity

$= \dfrac{Coupon(\$)}{(1 + interest\ rate)}$

$= \dfrac{Coupon(\$)}{(1 + interest\ rate)^2}$

$= \dfrac{Coupon(\$)}{(1 + interest\ rate)^3}$

Sum of the above equals the present value of an annuity formula:

$$PV = PMT \times \left[\dfrac{1 - (1 + i)^{-n}}{i} \right]$$

Where: PV = Present Value
PMT = Coupon Payment
i = Interest rate
n = Number of periods

V_{BOND} = sum of PVs

This equation looks great on a blackboard, but you don't have to carry around a financial calculator to utilize this concept. Instead, you can use an online calculator to do the exact same thing as the example above. Maybe you are considering buying a $1,000.00 bond that will pay $100.00 a year for 5 years, with a 10% coupon. (Again 10% is rare, but works for this example)

You can use an online present value calculator(www.investopedia.com/calculator/pvcal.aspx) to decipher the present value. In this example, that 1,000.00 in 5 years with a 10% *discount rate* it is worth $620.92 now. Therefore, if you can get more than $620.92 now then take that investment instead.

If you want to be an uber wonk and get insane with your speculations, then assume there is 2% inflation and use the Net Present Value (NPV) calculator and you will see that the future value of the investment may be the same nominal value, but have less purchasing power (i.e. The cost of what you were saving for went up). As you can see this is a giant wormhole that you can easily get sucked into. The information you have learned so far is good enough that you don't need to drive yourself mad.

The other thing pros do, that you don't need to is credit risk modeling. Rather than put together a team of analysts, you can go through a few quality testing steps on your own. Depending on the type of bond you are investing in there will be various sources to use for research. Some of the tools in the previous chapters will work well for this. The basic criteria you should be concerned with for any bond or debt instrument are these things:

1. What is the default risk
2. Do you anticipate any credit downgrades
3. Spreads (wide or narrow)
4. Opportunity cost

To find out more about any publicly traded corporation you can go to go to NASDAQ or Yahoo Finance. There you can key in the firm's name and easily find the public filings which allow you to learn everything about the firm and use the materials provided to crunch their numbers. Within the 10K you can find tons of valuable information that you can use as a research catalyst to determine if the firm is stable.

There are numerous things you can do to evaluate the credit quality. However, you must also look at the offering itself. Each bond will have something unique about it, so it is worth doing some auxiliary analysis. The most basic things to look for when researching a bond are:

1. <u>Covenant Analysis</u>: Provisions that establish rules and guidelines. There are 2 general types of covenants:

a. <u>Affirmative Covenants</u>: The issuer promises to do certain things.

b. <u>Negative (restrictive) Covenants</u>: These require the issuer does not take certain actions. (Like taking on more debt) Often there is a *maintenance test*, which requires the borrower's ratio of earnings available for interest to be a certain minimum figure on set reporting dates.

2. Collateral Analysis: Corporate debt can be secured or unsecured. Absolute priority does not always mean exclusive rights. There are usually some negotiations and depending on the significance of the firm's troubles there may be other rights (like taxes).

3. Ability to Pay Analysis: Assessing the issuer's ability to pay by business risk, governance risk and financial risk is also key.

Revenue and expenditures are uncertain and dependent on a myriad of factors. *Business risk* is defined as the risks associated with operating cash flows. To assess business risk you must consider the industry characteristics, company position, product/portfolio, peer group comparisons, regulatory environment, management quality, industry trends, risk appetite, technology, cost efficiency, strategic and/or operational competence. These factors are essentially the recipe that the big three (S&P, Moody's, Fitch) rating firms use to apply their credit rating.

Governance risk involves the ownership structure, management practices, and disclosure policies. Assessing the firms internal control systems and best practices is somewhat subjective. However, if you read on their 10Q that there is a concentration of influence by external stakeholders or a major board shake up this may spell problems.

Financial risk is assessing the quality of a firm's financial statements and identifying its trends. There are dozens of financial metrics and ratios that can be applied to a firm's balance sheet and income statement. The most popular are *interest coverage ratio* (how many times the interest is covered), *leverage ratio* (debt level), *operating cash flow* (income minus depreciation), *free cash flow* (operating cash flow minus expenditures), and *working capital* (assets minus liabilities).

ACTION ITEM

Hopefully, this chapter was not too overwhelming. It was not meant to confuse, trick, or intimidate you. The information provided should be just enough to pique your interest and spark your curiosity. Much of which, is very brief. The concepts of this chapter could be an entire book of its own. By explaining these fundamentals this should encourage you to do some exploring on the internet to enhance your knowledge on the topics that interest you.

The concepts in this chapter are much more complex than the other chapters. Performing due diligence is time consuming and can be difficult. No matter if you are a beginner or a professional no investment decision has a guarantee. Overall, the material presented here is something that will help you feel more confident about your investment choices. It will also give you some good questions to ask your portfolio manager.

If you prefer to only have investment grade, low risk bonds into your portfolio, then learning some advanced due diligence may be a giant waste of your time. If not, then the action item for this chapter is to use the information in this chapter to develop whatever version of due diligence that allows you to make good diversification decisions.

How can you develop your own methods that fit your investment objectives? A student once asked his guru, "How do you eat an elephant?" The guru paused as he reflected, and then calmly responded. *"One bite at a time."* Therefore, use your curiosity to study/learn a little bit at a time and then just build on that base of growing knowledge.

CONCLUSION

Growing up, my family never had any money. So, like most working class people, I learned how to manage money by barely having any. I also spent most of my early adulthood in poverty living the romanticized life of a starving artist. As an economically challenged person with no discretionary income I spent countless hours in the library. There, I poured over dusty books that smelled like stale cigarettes and open-dirt cemeteries. When I finally discovered the finance section, it fascinated me, and not just because I was poor. The velocity of money was just as amazing to me as it was confusing.

Despite my fascination with those basic finance books, I thought the information was purposely complex. In fact, because this was before the Internet era, I had to find other books to explain the ones that I was reading. That impenetrable material could have somehow been used to escape packed busses, third-hand clothes, and me wondering how I was going to find something decent to eat. Instead, I saw finance more as an intriguing puzzle than applicable or useful theory. So, I put this secret fascination with how the monetary system worked back on the shelf, because it seemed intangible.

Later in life, I embraced my fascination, got a job in back office operations at a bank, and then earned a business degree. Honestly, I did not care for the business model of banking, but I loved learning how to apply financial theory. It was there that I encountered an amazing life changing mentor who completely transformed me. This individual taught me a lot by pushing me out of my comfort zone, which eventually inspired me to get my MBA. In fact, all of the training I pursued allowed me to become a master of sucking up a waterfall of information and spitting out only what is necessary through a straw.

Please don't think I am bragging. Most of my friends constantly ask me to interpret market news, repair their business, or help them figure out how to deal with finance. They know I have dedicated a lot of time to learning that stuff, and I am always eager to help. Due to my background, I excel at helping regular people create the best future they can with the resources they have. So many people ask me to help them with personal finance that it has somehow become my life's mission, but in no way do I feel bad about this thankless task becoming a calling.

In fact, it makes me happy when I see other people succeed. What irritates me is when I see untrained financial gurus handing out inspirational cures instead of actual ones. This overwhelming flood of sagely profiteers and product peddlers is partially why I am writing my *Smart Money* series and selling each one for the price of a cup of coffee.

Rich people learn wealth management stuff from their wealthy parents, and sometimes assume it is their private family heirloom that is not to be shared. My goal is to take those same wealth management concepts and make them useful for everyone. Of course, everyone has individual goals so not everything in my books will be pertinent to you, but I believe everyone should have equal access. So, the mission of these books is to make these expensive secrets easy to use and understand.

Being suspicious mixed with cautious about any kind of credit, I have always avoided debt. When I read the 2015 studies about American debt, I was quite shocked. According to government statistics, the average American owes $7,281 in credit card debt and outstanding debt has risen to $3.4 trillion. To put this in perspective, in 2015 the GNP of Mexico was $1.9 trillion, the GNP of France was $2.5 trillion, and the GNP of the UK was 2.4 trillion. You can also easily combine the GDP of every Sub-Saharan country in Africa and still not even have half of the $3.4 trillion of American's outstanding debt.

In fact, if you want to be blown away, check out the *US debt clock.org*. Or go to the Federal Reserve *consumer credit site*. Without a doubt, debt is becoming an epidemic. With lower wages, and consumers having less discretionary income, prices for everything are rising just so businesses can remain open. If the current economic trends continue, credit will probably be harder to get. The people who are not feeling the pain are those who can borrow from themselves. You don't have to be in the 1% to do this, you just have to know how the system works, and be disciplined. How can the average person do this?

Most of my friends and family felt this same kind of pressure. After I explained some of the things I learned from being inside of the banking system and then simplified some complex financial theory for them, it made me happy to witness their pocketbook relief. Of course I cannot dissect every readers financial predicaments or status. However, what I can do is make books like this filled with a myriad of content so each person can pick and choose what is useful for them.

Throughout life, financial situations always change, so for every one of my personal finance books I made short chapters that can be read several times. I hope that you can find something new and useful to use each time your financial life changes and you read the books again. In the back of this book, I included some useful terms for beginners and also more advanced investors. So, make sure not to skip that section, because I think there is some awesome stuff in there.

ACTION ITEM

Take time out of your day to share what you know with someone. It does not matter what it is, as it will eventually be pertinent to them, and may even make their day. Plus, you might discover a new friend that you can interact with each day. If you liked this information and think it will help someone you know, then tell them about this book. After all, it is less than a Starbucks Frappucino. You could also pay it forward by posting a review for this book on Amazon or on Goodreads.

Before you go...

Thanks for reading. I hope you've enjoyed this book as much as I loved writing it. I appreciate every one of you for taking time out of your day or evening to read this. If you have an extra second, **I would love to hear what you think about it**. Please leave a comment on Amazon. To check out my other books, visit my Amazon page.

If you are interested in learning how the financial system works and how to use it to your advantage you may like the other book in this series, "*Smart Money: The Beginners Guide to Personal Finance*" is the easiest way to learn the basics about investing and finance. *"Smart Money: Wealth Building Strategies for Everyone"* will show you how to build you own bank. To learn some advanced active investor techniques try *Smart Money: Ten Proven Strategies that will Increase your Stock Market Returns.*

I have worked in finance for almost a decade, so these personal finance books are not like any other finance book you have read before. My goal with these books is to teach non finance professionals actionable finance concepts that they can use right away. With the books in this series I do my best to explain how the financial system really works in a simple yet detailed way.

Don't forget to check out the fundamental terms and also the resources section...

FUNDAMENTALS

Here are some basic terms for you to familiarize yourself with. Personal finance is not complicated, or impossible to understand, just laden with terminology. This section will help you immensely in understanding investment commentary and also serve to enhance your investment confidence and ability. It will also help you know what to look for and which tools or elements of your strategy that you need to read more about. Here are some of the more useful terms.

Affirmative Covenants: The issuer promises to do certain things.

Alternative Minimum Tax (AMT): A supplemental income tax imposed by the United States federal government required in addition to baseline income tax for certain individuals, corporations, estates, and trusts that have exemptions or special circumstances allowing for lower payments of standard income tax.

Annuity: (payment terms) Pays out a fixed stream of payments at agreed upon intervals.

Arbitrage: Buying or selling two separate securities to profit from the difference in their values or buying at one price and selling at another.

Ask: The current price to sell an asset.

Basis point: One hundredth of one percent, used chiefly in expressing differences of interest rates.

Balloon: (payment terms) Often bonds are issued to mature in intervals, bonds in a term issue that have the same maturity date are called balloon.

Bear Market: A market with declining valuations, which favors a "short" position where the investor profits from selling for a lower price than they paid for the investment.

Bid: The current price to buy an asset.

Bid Ask Spread: The difference between the buy and the sell price. Typically, the closer the spread is, the faster the stock is trading. A further apart spread means there is less volume and it will usually be harder to buy or sell.

Bull Market: A market in with rising valuation, which favors a "long" position where the investor profits from selling for a higher price than they paid for the investment.

Capital Gains: A gain realized by selling a stock, property or other asset; A capital loss is the opposite

Call provisions: It is not uncommon for an issuer to have the option to grant them the right to retire the issuance. This option is often detrimental to a bondholder's interests.

Call Risk: The issuer can choose to retire the bond at anytime

Commercial Paper: Short-term debt that matures in 270 days or less.

Committee on Uniform Securities Identification: (CUSIP) number that an investor can buy, each bond has an individual bond CUSIP number.

Compounding: Adding your gains back into your investment.

Convertible: (payment terms) Bonds like this can be converted to stock. A variation of this is where the bond can be exchanged for stock from a different firm (used in some mergers and acquisitions).

Coupon Rate: Interest the issuer agrees to pay each year is called the nominal rate, the coupon is the payments made to the owner during the term of the bond.

Covenant: Set of restrictions imposed on the borrower from the creditor. A covenant can be affirmative (do this) or negative (don't do this).

Default risk: is inherent in all bonds except treasury bonds--will the issuer have the cash to make the promised payments? Bonds are rated from AAA to D, and the lower the rating the riskier the bond, the higher its default risk premium, and, consequently, the higher its required ROI.

<u>Deflation:</u> This is a general decline in prices caused by a reduction in the supply of money. This is the opposite of inflation. In deflation, consumers wait to buy goods because they know the price will often go lower. (Quantitative Easing can change things; see definition)

<u>De Minimus Tax</u>: Only paid on munis bought at a discount more than 0.25% (income tax and capital gains on the discount).

<u>Discount</u>: A bond selling lower than face value.

<u>Double barreled bonds</u>: A hybrid supported by the municipalities creditworthiness and also project revenue.

<u>Exchange Trade Funds (ETF):</u> A "basket" of assets (stocks, bonds) that is designed to track a specific index.

<u>Event Risk</u>: Any significant event that disrupts the cash flow of the issuer.

<u>General Obligation Bonds</u>: A bond supported by taxation or the creditworthiness of the municipality.

<u>Flat Yield Curve</u>: When there is little or no variation between short and long term yields. It also implies, that demand and supply are similar across all yields and maturities.

<u>Income</u>: (payment terms) A rare arrangement where only

the face value of the bond is promised to be paid. Any coupon payments get paid only if the issuer has enough earnings to do so.

Interest Rate Risk: A bond's value typically falls as interest rates rise because its lower interest rates makes it less appealing to investors.

Interest only: (payment terms) The periodic payments are only the coupons, then at maturity the principal is paid off.

Inverted Yield Curve: (negative) Normally, an average investor will require more yield for longer durations. In this environment, yields are highest for short term maturities and decrease when maturity increases.

IRS Publication 550: The definitive resource for researching investment income taxes.

Liquidation Rights: Pre-established rules for paying off creditors during a bankruptcy or a default on debt.

Liquidity Risk: How fast a firm can come up with cash, or how much of their assets are available.

Maturity Date: The date that the bond principal is due to the creditor. Number of years until the bond matures and the issuer must repay the loan (return the par value)

Marketability Risk: Being unable to sell an asset or security due to low demand.

Muni: Municipal bond sold by cities to fund initiatives.

Mutual Fund: An investment vehicle where many shareholders pool their money in order to invest in a diversified portfolio of equities and bonds. A diversified conglomerate of group investments are chosen by a professional fund manager and statements of activity are issued.

Negative Covenants: (restrictive) These require the issuer does not take certain actions. (Like taking on more debt) Often there is a maintenance test, which requires the borrower's ratio of earnings available for interest to be a certain minimum figure on set reporting dates.

Nominal Yield: The interest rate (to par value) that the bond issuer promises to pay bond purchasers. This rate is fixed, applies to the life of the bond.

Over the Counter Market (OTC): The "yellow sheets" for bonds that have weekly bid and ask quotations on bonds that are restricted from trading on the open exchanges.

Par: A bond selling at face value.

Positive Sloped Yield Curve: (normal) Investors desire a higher rate of return for taking on risk for a longer period of time.

Premium: The amount above the list price or face value.

Perpetual: (payment terms) Like a stock dividend. This type of payment has no maturity date, is not redeemable, and has a steady stream of payments. (Also known as "perps") This kind of arrangement is rare because there are very few entities that are safe enough to issue bonds that will never be repaid.

Principal Value: (principal) amount issuer agrees to repay the bond holder at maturity date (also known as redemption value, par value or face value)

Put Provisions: This where the issuer has the option to change the maturity date of the bond. This allows the bondholder to sell the issue back at par value on designated dates. Here the advantage to the investor is that if interest rates rise after the issue date, thereby reducing the bond's price, the investor can force the issuer to redeem the bond at par value.

Revenue Bonds: A bond supported by revenue from a specific project.

Reinvestment Risk: The risk that you cannot find a similar yield at maturity.

Quantitative Easing: An unnatural injection of cash into the economic system to lower interest rates; In theory this should add money to the general economy, combined with the lower rates this should encourage borrowing, and spark inflation; However, if lending policies tighten this "extra" capital can skew the traditional economic balance of such an activity and cause market turmoil.

<u>Sector Risk</u>: Certain firms experience business cycle downturns.

<u>Sinking fund:</u> (payment terms) Periodic payments are made, but the issuer sets aside money in a separate custodial account for the exclusive purpose of retiring a portion of the bonds.

<u>Term to Maturity</u>: The number of years over which the issuer has promised to meet the conditions of the obligation.

<u>Treasury Bills</u>: "T-Bills" are short-term U.S Treasury bonds that mature within one year or less from the time of issuance (with maturities of 4, 13, 26, and 52 weeks)

<u>Treasury Notes</u>: "T-Notes" are U.S Treasuries with maturities of 1, 3, 5, 7, or 10 years and have a slightly higher yield than T-Bills.

<u>Treasury Bonds</u>: T-Bonds are offered with maturities of 10, 20 and 30 years. The ten year treasury is by far the most widely followed because it is used as both a benchmark for the treasury market and also as a basis for the banks to calculate mortgage rates.

Unsecured Bonds: Have a "junior" claim on the assets. Bankers call this a subordinate debenture. In the case of default, junior claims are subordinate to those of other bond holders.

Variable Rate: (payment terms) The coupon *floats* and is usually based on LIBOR or the Fed funds rate with a quoted spread added that is fixed.

Wash Sale: The term applies to the repurchase of shares within 30 days, which automatically disallows a loss for tax purposes.

Yield to Maturity: (YTM) The current bond yield is the rate of interest paid to the bond holder, and the yield to maturity is the total yield if it is held to maturity.

Zero Coupon Bond: No coupon, instead the investor buys at a discount and then gets paid the interest at the maturity date (the difference between the buy price and par value.

MUST READ "CLASSIC" FINANCE BOOKS:

(not ranked)

"Reminiscence of a Stock Operator"
By Edwin Lefevre

"The Theory of Investment Value"
By John Burr Williams

"Market Wizards"
By Jack Schwager

"Common Stocks and Uncommon Profits"
By Phil Fischer

"Against the Gods"
By Peter Bernstein

"Think and Grow Rich"
By Napoleon Hill

"Rich Dad Poor Dad"
By Robert Kiosaki

"The Intelligent Investor"
By Benjamin Graham

"When Genius Failed"

By Roger Lowenstein

"Security Analysis"
By Benjamin Graham and David Dodd

"The Handbook of Fixed Income Securities"
By Frank J. Fabozzi

"The Essays of Warren Buffett"
By Warren Buffett

"Liar's Poker"
By Michael Lewis

"A Random Walk Down Wall Street"
By Burton Malkiel

"Traders, Guns, and Money"
By Satajit Das

NOTE: Find these, and read them. Every single book on this list is available for the cost of a library card.

ABOUT THE AUTHOR

John Endris is a full blown business geek who earned a
Bachelor of Science in Business and an MBA from St.
Mary's University. He is a business strategy advisor, a
serial entrepreneur, active investor, and has an extensive
background in the financial services industry.

NOTES:

NOTES:

NOTES:

Made in the USA
Monee, IL
31 October 2024

69064194R00080